D1565158

CM:

DEVELOPING, MARKETING, AND DELIVERING CONSTRUCTION MANAGEMENT SERVICES

CM:

DEVELOPING, MARKETING, AND DELIVERING CONSTRUCTION MANAGEMENT SERVICES

Charles B. Thomsen

President, The CRS Group, Inc., Houston, Texas

McGRAW-HILL BOOK COMPANY

New York   St. Louis   San Francisco   Auckland
Bogotá   Hamburg   Johannesburg   London   Madrid   Mexico
Montreal   New Delhi   Panama   Paris   São Paulo
Singapore   Sydney   Tokyo   Toronto

720.68
TH8c

Library of Congress Cataloging in Publication Data

Thomsen, Charles B.
  CM: developing, marketing, and delivering construction management services.

  Includes index.
  1. Construction industry—Management.
  2. Engineering—Management. I. Title.
  HD9715.A2T49   624′.068   81-2722
                                       AACR2

4 5 6 7 8 9 0   KP KP   8 9 8 7 6 5

ISBN 0-07-064490-X

The editors for this book were Joan Zseleczky and Richard Mickey, the designer was Elliot Epstein, and the production supervisor was Teresa F. Leaden. It was set in Electra by Bi-Comp, Incorporated.

Printed and bound by The Kingsport Press.

CONTENTS

Acknowledgment

This book is the product of many years of companywide thought and discussion on the nature of construction management. Our ideas inspired memos, which in turn became reports, which then evolved into in-house books and promotional pieces. Thanking all of the people who contributed to this effort would be impossible: there are so many people who helped in so many ways. But I must extend my gratitude to the officers of CM Inc. during my years there: Gus Akselrod, Mo Appleton, Larry Bickle, Robert Cooke, Warren Dean, Jack Eimer, Robert Finley, Glenn Hobratschk, Perry King, John Littlejohn, Tandy Lofland, John Loyd, Charlie Martini, David Necker, Bob Reisacher, Joseph Scarano, Tom Shishman, Byron Stenis, David Thomas, and Frank Whitcomb. Bill Caudill, Tom Bullock, Herb Paseur, Nick Kolesnikoff, and John Focke, officers of our affiliate companies in The CRS Group, Inc., also made effective criticisms. Special thanks go to Melva Payne for her support, to Paule Hewlett for her fine editorial insight, and, of course, to my wife Lois, for her surgical precision in reviewing grammar and clarity of thought.

Charles B. Thomsen

January 1981

CM:

DEVELOPING, MARKETING, AND DELIVERING CONSTRUCTION MANAGEMENT SERVICES

1

SELLING CM SERVICES

Although it may not be a matter of policy, every person in a company is responsible for sales. Through performance, appearance, and manners everyone affects the top line. Why? Because in construction management, as in most other businesses, many sales are repeat work or expanded scope, a result of doing good jobs. And because reputations get around fast: it's hard to get new clients without happy old ones. Also, because people judge an entire company by their contact with only a few individuals. The look of an office, the character of a field team, the way secretaries treat people on the phone—these all form an impression of the company for the public.

So, everyone in the company must be *sales-conscious*. Whenever a competitor hires "salesmen," I'm delighted. By setting up a marketing department, isolated from the company's operations, the competitor is creating a distinction that ignores what actually sells. Good work is what sells, whether it's a secretary, a scheduler, a sales representative, or a vice president doing the good work. Such individuals' reputations quickly become one with their company's.

But not even the finest reputation will bring new clients knocking on the door. A few firms have endured indefinitely with just a few clients and their continuous building programs, but most companies must seek out new clients as well as keeping old clients happy. And getting new clients is hard work, requiring initiative, vigor, imagination, and specialization.

Because it's so hard and so critical, getting new clients should be the primary responsibility of a company's senior officers, operating with the full support of the entire firm. Here's why:

• *People who hire construction managers are decision makers; they want to talk to other decision makers.* They won't accept lightweights who don't understand the business or who lack authority to make commitments.

Once a junior staff member and I were talking to a potential client about doing a difficult job. I was willing to promise quick delivery, but he was reluctant to commit to anything but a safe, sure schedule. My first reaction was that his sales instincts were poor, but I soon realized what was behind the difference in our approaches. As the president, I knew I could mobilize the company's efforts for an unusual effort. He was unsure.

• *It's hard to direct attention to a new project.* By their very nature, companies are burdened by inertia. They tend to do what they have done, what they are doing, what they do best. The sales representative must have both the responsibility and the clout to get the company moving on a new project—perhaps with new staff and a variation of basic services.

• *Sales shape a company's future.* What you sell is what you do—so getting work should be the responsibility of key officers. And it's a two-way street: those who know the market should steer an organization.

Too many people think they can decide what services they want to provide and then hire people to sell them. That's backward. Ideas for new products and services come from people who know the market. I've been told that both pool sweeps and weed eaters were invented by salespeople, not engineers.

Even if you did find a way to put sales in the hands of junior people, it wouldn't be long before they were running the company. They would find new clients and shape operations to support their promises. The person selling to the client represents a professional services company. If that person does not really represent the power behind those services, problems are going to result.

To a client, a building is a problem. What a construction manager has to sell is solutions. And just as no two problems are identical, neither are the solutions—a company's services have to be tailored for each job. Sellers need imagination and a good understanding of how the system works to adjust their approach for special clients.

But sales is not a job for loners or prima donnas. It takes teamwork and brainstorming that may involve the whole company. For example, it may be that your estimator is so obviously good that everyone your company does business with is impressed. That kind of skill will help bring you work. And while most successful companies have had a particularly successful salesperson, no company's growth should be limited by the number of prospects one man or one woman can court. Gone are the days when charisma won jobs: clients are too smart. They want to talk to the people they will be working with.

The officers who are involved in sales can't turn their backs on operations, especially during the start-up phase of a new project. Here are five good reasons why:

1 The beginning stage of a project is crucial, no time for a handoff. The person who understands the new job is the one who sold it. If promises aren't kept, both the sales agent and the company will have an unhappy client and a bad reference.

2 If an officer ignores a client after the contract is signed, word will get around that the company has a shill in its top management, and that verdict will be right.

3 A creative seller often promises a prospective client new services that the company has not provided before. The special solution to the special problem must be carefully managed, or the company will fall back into its standard routine. Innovation requires attention from the top to succeed.

4 Unless they stay involved, salespeople will lose touch with the company's evolving capabilities, which will weaken their ability to sell them.

5 And finally, no officer can be a complete leader without supporting all the company's goals, which invariably must include performance and profit as well as growth.

QUALIFYING PROSPECTS

Leads come from clients, employees, the *Commerce Business Daily*, colleagues, and advertising—rarely from reading the newspaper. By the time a project gets there it's too late.

Architects can be a solid source of leads for a construction manager. In our early days at CM Inc. we never thought we'd get jobs from architects because we assumed they wouldn't want to work with a competitor's (CRS') affiliate. But over half our work has come from architects, and some of CRS' biggest competitors, firms like Hellmuth, Obata & Kassabaum and Perkins & Will, have brought us into projects. Again, it boils down to a company's reputation—at one point the value of your services outweighs professional jealousy.

But usually the problem is not too few leads, it's too many. There is an ancient Chinese proverb, "Do not try to catch two frogs with one hand." It applies to sales. It makes no sense to pursue a project unless you are prepared to expend maximum effort. If you don't, you'll lose to someone who does. Salespeople should pick targets carefully and go after them full speed. Exclusive choices improve the hit rate, save time and money, and maximize the whole company's sales efforts.

But it takes a strong will to reject opportunity, no matter how slim. Once we uncovered a prospect who didn't seem in a hurry, who had no understanding of construction management, and whose architect was leery of our affiliation with CRS. He hedged and waffled when we talked to him; he didn't want to be pressured into any decisions. I can't believe, now, that it actually took some thought before we decided to forget it and apply our efforts elsewhere. And I still can't believe how rarely we make these obvious decisions.

Because construction management is a relatively new service, we run into curiosity seekers—underworked staff members of public agencies who decide it's time to bone up on CM. Much money and effort can be wasted preparing proposals and flying across the country when there isn't any project. So how do you know if a lead is real? There are some telltale questions to ask.

• Is the project funded? If not, how will it be funded?

• Does construction management really make sense for the project?

• Are the decision makers convinced that the idea is good?

• Does another firm have the inside track?

Something to always watch out for is a situation where one company is set up—included in the selection process just to give the appearance of objective decision making or to make sure the favored company keeps its price down. The better a company's reputation, the better qualified it is for the supporting role of fall guy.

On one extremely large hospital job we pursued, we called on the best local contractor to discuss a joint venture. We learned he had already joined up with a national firm—an excellent company that is one of our toughest competitors. When we visited the client we heard this competitor's sales rhetoric and saw his brochures.

The giveaway was the interview. For this giant job they had scheduled eight firms to be interviewed in one day with the decision immediately after. As with most jobs, the project was in the bag long before the interview. We shouldn't have wasted our time.

No Thanks

There aren't many good ways to say no on those occasions when a job doesn't look just right for your company. And dangers are inherent in every decline. Rejection, especially to a potential client, is hard to swallow; and you should be aware of what the repercussions might be.

• "We're committed to the hilt and could not provide you with the resources you need on the project." (*Danger:* The next client you want could hear you're too busy.)

• "Our fees would be higher than our competition's on this job." (*Danger:* You can be labeled expensive.)

• "XYZ would really be more appropriate for this particular work." (This is probably the best approach.)

The best way to avoid having to say "no thanks" is to search for first-class business and real prospects. It's something of a cycle, as first-class prospects usually want a construction manager that works for first-class clients. A company is known by the company it keeps. Avoid the flaky ones.

HOMEWORK

Goethe said, "Nothing is more terrible than to see ignorance in action." He could have been on the way home from a bad CM presentation. Watching an officer at an interview for a big job fumbling for answers, praying for inspiration, and struggling to sound confident is embarrassing for everyone. The only way to avoid this type of torture is to do your homework.

Once a prospect looks real and worthwhile, the best thing to do is find out everything you can about the project, the client, the architect-engineer (A-E), and the community. There are traditional sources of business information that are always helpful: Dun & Bradstreet, annual reports, market analysts' research data. But don't stop there. You can sometimes call clients and tell them you'd like to meet with them to learn more about their projects. Most clients appreciate directness, and because their project is important to them, they probably want to discuss their concerns.

Architects are another source of information; and while they may not be able to give you the job on a platter, they sure can keep you from getting it. The architect probably wants to know that you'll be a team player and that you take pride in supporting good design. Any experience your company has had with other architects will show that the company understands what's involved in the design process, and should be used as a professional reference. And a construction manager's participation in award-winning design efforts is always impressive.

Most architects know the principles of construction management, but a little more education about your own company might help. You should stress the general advantages of the architect–construction manager relationship: We can make the architect's job easier and more profitable. But also explain how construction management can make the architect's job harder. Listing the pros and cons this way will establish your credibility and let you demonstrate your understanding of design problems.

On-Site Insight

Another critical part of the homework phase is inspecting the site. Your visit may trigger an idea or reveal a liability in the project that hasn't been thought of yet. Even if the trip doesn't furnish much new information (it usually won't), the client will appreciate your interest.

The best time to figure out the best way to do the job is before the presentation. Careful consideration of the alternatives and a realistic project-delivery approach will impress a client who's probably hearing pretty standard hard sells at this point from the competition. Look for the clear, simple truth; it's hard to find, but it sure is easy to sell.

The Decision Point

Sometimes the client's decision makers are hard to identify and harder still to reach. Sometimes they are protected by a technical staff that diverts a potential construction manager's attention. There is always the risk of spending time selling to a technical staff not involved in the final decision. And there are always exceptions. Sometimes a technical staff has either the authority to make the final decision or the confidence of an executive that wants to delegate the decision.

Often a way to get to the top exists even if a technical staff is directly involved, provided it's all out in the open. On a state government job where selection was apparently the responsibility of the technical staff, I called the state architect and asked him two qualifying questions: "Can an out-of-state firm really get this job?" and "What are you looking for?" The state architect appreciated my directness. His response was yes to the first question, and his answer to the second jived with what his staff was telling us. (In my own mind, I believe that the state architect went to some length to make sure we had a fair shot at the job after he had assured us that we did. Had we not asked, he might not have felt so compelled.) We got the job. But I had carefully made a point of telling the technical manager I was going to call so he would not feel slighted.

Clients want to get to know their prospective construction managers. They don't want to hire people they don't like. And you should want to get to know your client to make sure you can keep the working relationship friendly. Business ventures are rarely successful when one party feels the other is unethical or misguided, and it's hard to do good work for clients you don't like. During the homework phase it's a great advantage to gain the confidence of a principal decision maker. You need someone who can tell you and keep you informed about the project's hidden agenda. The conventional priorities of time, cost, and quality are always packaged between an owner's other objectives. Some hidden-agenda items are fairly common. For instance:

• A client may want bid packages structured to maximize participation by local contractors, minority contractors, union (or nonunion) contractors, etc. Or the client may want to bring in outside competition to break up price fixing.

• A client may want a construction manager to absorb some of the responsibility and to minimize the risk if there are any problems. On the other hand, the client may be a bit of a risk taker and may want to take credit for the best possible results.

• If public money is involved, a key selling point may be cost predictability and budget containment, not necessarily economy. If it's private money, economy will probably be more important.

• Some clients place great value on professionalism, education, and sophistication; they want someone who understands advanced systems. Others view construction as a tunnel of horrors, and what they want is a tough construction manager with mud on his boots to protect them on the way through.

• Some clients want to relinquish responsibility for the project and get involved only in critical decisions. Others view the project as a major event in their lives, and they want to be directly involved, perhaps with the construction manager operating as an extension of their own staff.

There are more of these hidden-agenda issues that are equally typical; still, every job reveals new ones. If you are aware of them you'll know which capabilities to stress at the interview.

Listen and Learn

You can learn a lot during the information-gathering stage that will help you sell your services later on. It's a mistake at this point to overwhelm board members or members of the selection committee with a hard sell of your company. It will be a turnoff and destroy rapport. Use the time to find out what business the client is in, what the buyer influences are, who the competition is, and who will be at the interview. This type of information is essential to building a good project-delivery concept and a good selling strategy. You can use this information to demonstrate at the interview how responsive and flexible your company's services can be.

It's unprofessional to sell construction management before there is a clear picture of the client's needs and constraints. Selling *what is needed* will get jobs and keep the company developing with the times.

In the days before CM Inc. was founded, I went to Maryland for CRS to give a community college board a presentation. It was going well. Heads were nodding in agreement. But late in the presentation, when I spoke about working with the college faculty, the heads stopped nodding. What was wrong? It was our standard pitch, which is still true: We like working with faculties because it helps us design good schools. I figured they had missed the point so I repeated it. More blank looks, so I really hit it hard: "Your faculty knows what a good college is, not your architect! We just can't do a good job without your faculty!"

Finally there was a response from the board's president. "I'm sorry to hear that, Mr. Thomsen. We don't plan to hire a faculty until construction is nearly complete." We didn't get the job. Had I done my homework, we might have had a chance to take a fresh approach to community college design.

Strengths and Weaknesses

After the homework is done, but before the proposal or the interview, get together with the other team members and brainstorm, to identify the company's strengths and weaknesses in relation to the project and in comparison with the competition's. It's important to specify and document how and why you're good. In this situation, the more thought, the better; the strategies get stronger as they're worked through.

Knowing who the competition is and what it stands for can crystallize a company's strong points. You have to be careful of statements like "We're housing specialists—we've done dozens of housing projects" if your competition has done hundreds. A company must always sell relative strengths, those capabilities that are actually superior to the competition's. When we get together, someone always says, "Well, we're just better at our job." Phooey—all of us think we're better. This is a very hazardous time for delusions of grandeur or any kind of pretense. Neither one can help sell a company. Clients are smart. Generalities like "We have worked around the world on every type of building project" can get you into trouble. Claims should be specific and accurate.

When up against stronger competition, it may boil down to a "we try harder" pitch. There's nothing wrong with that, and sometimes it works.

JOINT VENTURES

Some people think that joint ventures are formed because one company decides that it is compatible with another and that the services they offer are complementary. Some people think a company forms a joint venture to get someone to share the risk or to increase its own capability for a big project. But the only real reason to form a joint venture is to get the job. Few joint ventures would exist if one of the companies had been sure it could get the job by itself.

The most common joint venture in the CM industry is one that combines a respected local company with a famous national one. Many clients, particularly those from the public sector, are torn between selecting national and selecting local businesses. They want the best talent available anywhere—but they also feel they should return tax revenues to the community, they feel comfortable with local people, and they feel that a local firm will put out extra effort to maintain its reputation.

These ambivalent feelings must be respected. They are honest and sensible. And joint ventures—by combining the strengths of two or more companies—can usually be responsive to most clients' particular needs. If a large firm with international experience can form a joint venture with a local firm, that combination will offer the client the best of both worlds.

There are exceptions to this standard around-the-world–around-the-corner theme. One of our clients wanted to staff part of the project team and act as our joint venture partner himself. Another client felt we would be more objective about local subcontractors and suppliers without a local partner. In a third instance the client wanted all the local contractors left in the market to bid on the work.

Qualifying associates is sometimes more difficult than qualifying leads. Contractual liabilities are involved, and besides, within each joint venture lies a potential compromise of each company's ever-precious reputation. Certain qualities and standards, though, can be used to screen for potential joint venture partners.

When we look for associates, we look for contractors who negotiate work. We look for a company with an organization, not a team with only one player. We search for pride, an establishment image, and a professional reputation. We also prefer 50-50 deals. If one company has a junior position, its officers will feel buffered from any real responsibility. They won't give the relationship or the project their after-hours concern. If it's 50-50, each partner will be more likely to be committed to the project's success.

Good potential partners can be found in every major American city. They are usually investors in the city and board members of its institutions. They can bring you in on new jobs and improve your chances of winning them. They also deliver high-quality work and can frequently help you make yours better. Joint ventures, properly conceived and managed, can provide many mutual benefits.

PRESENTATIONS

Clients in the market for construction managers almost always schedule a presentation into the selection process. Not to learn about the company, because corporate facts can be best communicated in typed facts and figures. Clients want to know whether they will like the proposed CM team and whether they can work with it. So human qualities like personality, character, integrity, intelligence, and affability are the merchandise being examined. But in no way will personality or a hotshot presentation suffice for well-planned project strategies and creative delivery methods. It's essential to make sense and show you know your stuff. No one can get the job on sincerity alone.

First cuts are usually made on the basis of written proposals. By the time of the interview the client's choice is limited to a few firms, all of which seem able to do the job—so the competition may be a process of elimination. The client might be looking for reasons *not* to hire you.

The Presentation Team

Most clients want to see the team that will do the job at the presentation. After all, the team consists of people they will be working with for a considerable amount of time. This presents some tricky problems for national firms. First, not many CM companies have people sitting around on their hands; and while most clients think they're going to get started on their project right after the interview, few actually do. Second, good project managers and superintendents are often action-oriented people, and their field language may be out of place at an interview. Third, for a national company, picking a project team involves moving families. If every potential move were negotiated with the entire project team for every job on a company's development list, most of the staff and their families would be kept in a constant state of emotional shock.

On one project we decided that we'd explain these problems to our client, give him typical résumés to review, and explain that if we got the job, we'd pick the team. We didn't get the job—a firm that presented a "real" project team did. There's no canned solution to this staffing problem. The answers will have to be arrived at on a project-by-project basis.

Some companies have a neat solution: They lie through their teeth. They put together a great-looking project team to present at the interview, with little intention of actually assigning the same people to the project. When the project schedule invariably slips after selection, they have an excuse to restaff. Although this approach seems to work for some, I think it's a lousy idea. In order to make it work, you must ask your staff to lie to your potential client. You shouldn't ask them to be deceptive for the company, nor should they agree to be.

But sometimes you will have to play brinkmanship on this issue. On one project in the Rocky Mountains we chose one of our outstanding superintendents to present as part of the project team. One hitch: He had never been west of Maryland and he was justifiably concerned about how he would like it.

There wasn't time to send him out there for a trial run. We told him to assume he'd love it and commit to the move at the interview. He did and we got the job. He also loves the West so much now he swears he'll never leave—which worked out great at the time but will probably make a problem if we want to move him back east for the next job.

A couple of general presentation strategies can take the emphasis off the *need* for a preassigned project team. Any project that takes 3 years to complete will have personnel turnover; potential clients should be told about the company's talent on the bench. Let them know the other things beyond the project team that make up a good company: advanced computer systems, financial strength, organized teamwork for problem solving, good management, and procedures for project initiation, audits, and closeouts.

On any presentation team it's critical to match the performers with the audience—brass with brass, staff with staff. The president and general manager of a construction management firm might overpower a staff interview team; conversely, a presentation to the president of a potential client's company should be given by your top executives. There is also great danger in outnumbering the client. A common tendency is to take too many people to an interview, particularly when joint ventures are involved. The presentation team should be limited to the key performers.

Rehearsals are important for the interview team. The presentation has to look coordinated, friendly, sharp. Everyone should watch and listen to the speaker, laugh at the others' jokes, and be careful not to restate points others have made, qualify their arguments, or correct them. Obvious respect for each other is the first step toward gaining the client's respect.

As part of the rehearsal, you should time the presentation, going over it several times. A video recorder can show you what your personal strengths and weaknesses are better than any audience can. And presentations, just like everything else, respond to hard work; they get better.

Style and Content

The greatest temptation in an interview is to talk too much about your own company. Poor clients—they are a captive audience for us to bore with endless slides of our pet projects. It's more effective to talk about a client's project: Clients are more interested in *their* problems and opportunities. On any presentation rehearsal, check to see if you use "we" more than "you," and if you use your company name more than your client's.

Still, you have to explain your company's expertise. How do you do it? Wallie Scott, of CRS, a consummate salesman, developed this technique: He would categorize the client's challenges and show slides illustrating some of CRS' solutions on other projects, allowing that they might not be applicable in the client's case. He found a way to talk about the client's project and his own company's experience simultaneously.

Basic building blocks are useful for developing a presentation, but it's important to avoid canned monologues. The most impressive presentation is one that sounds fresh; it's hard to sound enthusiastic about old ideas. You can talk about the new ideas the company is enthusiastic about and the special characteristics of the project at hand. Enthusiasm is contagious, too—if the presentation team sounds interested, the client will get caught up in the spirit. The atmosphere will be much more friendly and much more conducive to good communication.

Case Histories

Most construction management presentations are beefed up with slides and with "case histories," pieces that show and describe the company's favorite projects. These are standard promotional materials, and they have their value. But both slides and case histories are overused (which makes them boring) and ill-used (which can make them dangerous). All material of this sort should be carefully screened for applicability to both the audience and the project. Only those that relate directly to the project at hand in either size, type, or location should be used. And the parallels between the two should be clearly drawn.

Once a vice president and I were interviewing for a project with a budget of about $300 million. We hit them with a case history for a $3 billion project and ten minutes of hyperbole about our experience with some of the world's largest construction management jobs.

One of the men said, "With all of those big projects, are you interested in our little $300 million job?" They thought they had the biggest project around. We popped their balloon. They hired another firm. That popped ours.

The only place to use a famous project is in the introduction. "You can perhaps identify our company as the company that did so-and-so," a point which also conveys the idea of continuity and heritage.

It's natural to be more enthusiastic and more knowledgeable about projects you were personally involved in. Beware: Pride can distort a clear view. It's important to guard against using case histories just because someone on the team has a story to tell. What clients want is an objective, knowledgeable comparison between the challenges presented in the completed project and the challenges they face.

Faking It

During the homework phase you'll pick up on the client's attitudes about the project. And while addressing those attitudes and speaking to them is essential to a good presentation, it's equally important to stop short of parroting back what the client wants to hear. I'll say it again: Clients are smart. They can recognize phonies. It's possible to get hired even if a client doesn't agree with everything you say in the presentation, but it becomes almost impossible the minute you're caught faking.

It's a matter of judgment whether to disagree and try to alter a client's thinking about some aspect of the project at this early stage of the game; but it has been done, successfully, after some careful groundwork has been laid and some strong arguments presented. The thing to guard against is sounding brash, opinionated, or inflexible. Who knows? You may need to reconsider your position, with the client's values in mind. Many construction management services that are now routine were initially developed to solve a client's unusual problem.

It's important to make it obvious that every idea you present has been carefully considered and organized. Let the client know you did your homework. It will help demonstrate convincingly that you want the job, you have initiative, and you are a professional.

As a construction manager, your job is to make even the most complex, difficult project into a building program that sounds realistic, achievable, even simple. It's the same with most professionals. When I see Segovia playing the guitar it looks like something I could do myself. And while the idea isn't to suggest that the client can handle it alone, there is some use in making clear that you're confident that the project can be a success.

Clients in the market for construction managers are looking for solidity, stability, and someone who will manage their money conservatively. These qualities can best be presented by showing how a company has retained clients and grown on repeat work and by discussing how different kinds of work have broadened the company's knowledge and supported the development of high-technology management systems. This would be the place to talk about your company's low personnel turnover, and about the background and development of the firm. If your company is active in professional societies or participates in educational programs, the client should know. But throughout the presentation you have to be careful not to come off sounding too academic, too high-tech, or like a stuffy professional. A client hires a construction manager to be practical.

Placement

The two favored spots in the presentation sequence are first and last, and your presentation should be designed according to your position. In the first slot, the idea is to define the primary issues in the project and demonstrate how well your company fits. Other firms will then be measured by your yardstick. In the last position there is the advantage of being the best-remembered. Previous interviews educated the client's team, and they're tired of hearing about the past experience of every company. You can skip the academics and come on like gangbusters, addressing the major issues and showing how you really are better than anyone else.

The middle spot is the worst. Sandwiched amid all the competition, there's real pressure to do something memorable. Bill Caudill of CRS, who stuttered in his youth, once opened a presentation by saying, "I under-st-stand you are giving each ar-architect thi-thirty minutes for his presentation. I st-st-stutter. You should give me fo-forty five." He got the job.

Personality

People tend to hire people who are like themselves. An industrial psychologist once had me describe the ideal CM Inc. employee; then he asked how this ideal employee differed from the way I would describe myself. I couldn't think of one difference. Clients also look for people with similar styles and values. There are all kinds of mannerisms and outward clues to a person's lifestyle—clothes, haircut, tone of voice, degree of formality. Even if you don't want to dress by your client's dress code, take care that your own doesn't become alienating. That's a crazy way to lose a job.

Another crazy way is to outsmart a client. I once heard this memorable exchange: "The worst thing you can do is tell a guy he's wrong," countered by "No, the worst thing is to tell a guy he's wrong and prove it."

Most clients don't really understand the jargon used in the construction business; the truth is that most of *us* don't really understand the jargon used in the construction business. People who really know what they are talking about say it so others can understand. For the sake of clarity, don't fuzz up the issues with technical-sounding lingo. Everyday words work better.

You don't get much CM work by being a hotshot entertainer. I've had many prospective clients congratulate me on making the best presentation—*after* they'd hired another firm. What you're after is the chuckle, not the belly laugh. But don't be afraid to be humorous about the content of your presentation. When Joe Scarano, now president of CM Inc., tells people that we coined the term "fast-track," he always adds, "We thought we ought to take credit for that; everyone else does."

Funny thing, though: Humor can work against you if you sacrifice your dignity for a laugh. When we interviewed with Disney we tucked in a slide of two of us in hard hats pasted up with Mickey Mouse ears. We flashed the slide on the screen, and we got a great laugh. Somebody else got the job.

The Scene

The environment for the presentation is incredibly important. It should be as comfortable and as flattering to your team as possible. You can take fate in hand and make it so with a little preparation. Someone on the team should visit the location and check out the room, locate the light switches, find the electrical outlet you need, and figure out where to put the slide projector and where you ought to stand. Prior to the interview, one of CM Inc.'s top officers likes to get the feel of a room, talk out loud to hear his voice, and get familiar with the new surroundings. A lot of janitors have been sold on our company in the process.

You want to be able to check for audience reaction, so see if there's a way to dim the room without plunging it into total darkness. Once we held up a presentation for five minutes to bring in a lamp to prevent total blackout. It was worth it.

Technique

There is only one approach to presentation technique: *Be yourself.* There's no point in memorizing or adopting a particular pose. After you've figured out the best way to do the job and assembled the best team to do it, all you have to do is be transparent. And since so few of us are good actors, you have to follow your own natural style. Nerves get in everybody's way; if you're unsure and inarticulate, that makes your client uncomfortable. The surest way to cure a case of nerves is to be forthright and honest about your presentation and your delivery. This means admitting when you don't know the answer to a question and owning up to a mistake the company may have made in the past.

I used to be insecure about being an architect–construction manager rather than a contractor–construction manager. At one of my first seminar presentations on construction management to a group of both architects and contractors, a tough old contractor got up in the back of the room and said, "Mr. Thomsen, some of what you said about construction made sense, but I'm puzzled. You said you were with CRS. I've built some buildings for CRS. I didn't know anybody there knew *anything* about construction." At this, all the contractors and architects laughed very hard. Then he said, "As a matter of fact, I didn't think *any* architects knew anything about construction." Just the contractors laughed this time. Harder.

I never recovered my balance. The rest of the presentation is a blur; I'm sure it was a disaster. But later I used that story to begin all my presentations to architects and contractors. It served two purposes: First, it defused any professional jealousy in the audience and made my listeners feel more comfortable with me; second, it got me over my insecurities so I was more relaxed.

Top Ten

While the main thing is to be totally natural and totally transparent, there are some fundamental techniques that make for a good presentation. Here are ten:

1 *Focus.* Don't look over the heads of the audience. Make eye contact and hold it on one person per point. Don't slip from face to face in the middle of a thought.

2 *Be natural.* Stiff, wooden phrases like "We are honored to have been invited to present our qualifications for this distinguished project" create distance between the speaker and the audience. Real people don't talk like that. Measured informality, even with foreign clients, comes through as honesty. (Make sure, though, to keep the tone informal rather than overfamiliar—that's insulting.)

3   *Use humor.* But don't clown or act dopey, cute, or dirty. Wallie Scott can get away with telling a mildly off-color joke because he's such a clean-cut, wholesome guy; I'm scared to try it.

4   *Don't fidget.* But you can change your position after a point is made, to physically indicate that a new paragraph is coming. Watch your hands; avoid awkward or unnatural gestures that will distract the audience.

5   *Be aware of individuals.* In our business, skillful selling means making someone view the problem and the solution as we do. To make sure your strategy is working and your arguments are convincing, you need feedback from the audience. Body language is the best kind of feedback: if you're making your point, people will nod at you; if not, they'll lean back on their chairs and fold their arms. Involve people in your presentation until you get the right signals going, and keep them involved. If someone quits paying attention, address the next remarks directly to that person.

6   *Change pace.* Vary the volume of your voice, the rate of speech, and the length of pauses. Use vocal tools the way an artist uses color and proportion to emphasize certain points. And don't talk too fast— you may say something you haven't thought of yet.

7   *Use silence.* If there is a distraction in the room, such as serving of coffee, don't keep talking; wait it out. Pause after an important thought—silence can also be used to emphasize points.

Your silence can be particularly effective when someone asks an embarrassing question. First, you have a chance to think (many a job has been lost through a flip retort). Second, you appear to be looking for a sincere response, and that puts a damper on audience aggression. Third, often sympathy will go out to you before you answer, and a member of the audience will jump in on your side.

It's OK to be quiet and ponder a question. You don't have to think out loud; consider what you are going to say. Some of my colleagues have told me I never know how I feel about something until I hear what I have to say about it. Sad, but I'm afraid too often true.

8 *Plan your opening lines carefully.* You never get a second chance to make a first impression.

9 *Make it shorter.* A friend once pointed out to me that the Roman Catholic mass lasts a mere 20 minutes and has sold lots of people.

10 *Ask for the job.* Don't pussyfoot, but say clearly that you want the work. Say why in terms that will be meaningful to the client.

Questions and Answers

A beautifully organized presentation can fall apart at question-and-answer time. To keep the interview team from stumbling all over itself, it's a good idea to have one person field the questions. This person should direct attention to the appropriate team member, who should in turn respond to the question briefly. Too often we each feel compelled to get involved in every issue; thus a client asks a question and three people respond in sequence with three different answers. This generates confusion, destroys rapport, and, worst of all, indicates a lack of confidence in the other team members. It's annoying to see someone jump into an exchange with something like, "What Chuck is really trying to say is. . . ." If a question has been answered once, anything added by someone else had better be important.

You can tell how insecure a group is by the way it handles a question and the number of people who rush to answer it. On an interview for a large commercial job we were asked how big our field team would be. Our team hadn't discussed it before the presentation. Almost everyone carefully evaded the question and delivered a lengthy speech on the "CM Inc. Theory of Staffing a Project." What the client wanted to hear was an answer like "four."

When you're preparing for a presentation, it's essential to anticipate the negative questions. Then you can take the offensive and cover the answer during the interview. In a presentation for a civic center project, we discussed our experience with similar projects (we had done the estimating for four or five civic centers, but had never managed construction for one). During the presentation I should have said, "We have never provided full CM services on a civic center," and then gone on to illustrate how many of our "first" projects were great successes and how much of our experience was directly relevant. Instead I glossed over the issue. When it got to question time, I got it between the eyes: "Mr. Thomsen, how many civic centers have you done?" I looked silly. The board thought I was dissembling; I guess I was.

Incidents like that cause suspicion. The client may supposedly be using some objective checklist to evaluate the interviews, but it will be filled in *after* the interview. People react emotionally to situations and then build a structure of logic to support their emotional reaction. Again, if you are asked about an unsuccessful job or a weakness in your experience portfolio, be truthful. Explain how it happened and why. It sounds bad, but it also sounds honest and will give the rest of your presentation credibility.

The question-and-answer period is a time to relax and build friendships; it's not the time for more on-cue presentation. You should give your client a chance to talk without interruption.

There are questions that frequently come up; you should be prepared for them. While the questions are standard, the answers aren't. The appropriate answers have to be developed for each project. Here is a brief checklist of questions you'll probably hear during the selection process:

Questions about a Construction Manager's Replacing a General Contractor

- When some work is missed and not assigned to a contractor, who has the responsibility?

- What if there is a problem and it's not clear whom to pin it on? Who has the overall liability?

- Who does the work of the general contractor?

- How does a construction management firm that's not a contractor know what things cost?

- What contractors or subcontractors have you worked with?

Questions about a Construction Manager's Relationship with the Architect

- Who is responsible for quality?

- Does the architect have an edge? What if the architect wants to do one thing and the construction manager another? How do you get the architect to change the design?

- Isn't inspection (or programming, or project management) the responsibility of the architect?
- Who administers the guarantee period?

Questions on the Fast-Track—Multiple-Contract Concept

- Don't all those contracts mean more claims?
- How do I know what the final cost will be?
- What happens if one contractor damages another?
- How much money can your company save on a project? Is your fee an extra cost to the job?
- Aren't there more change orders with fast-track?

Questions Directed at a Nonlocal Firm

- Have you ever done a job here?
- How do you know what things cost here and how things are done?
- Are you familiar with local codes and construction practices?

Questions about the Company

- You are growing. Are you too busy to do the job?
- What's the smallest project you can do?
- How quickly can you staff our project?
- How many churches (or schools or hotels) have you built before?

- How often will I see you after the contract is signed?

- Would a little $20 million job get lost at your company?

- What is your batting average for bringing projects in on target?

- Who is assigned to our project?

- How can a young (or old) group of architects (or engineers) know anything about construction?

Leave-Behinds

Leave-behind material is used after a presentation to keep your presence felt. It may include several types of information:

- Names and titles of the presentation team.

- Address and phone number of a contact person at your company.

- An outline of the main topics of the presentation.

- A list of the major project issues.

- Excerpts from your submitted proposal, such as ten reasons why you are best for the job.

- Relevant article reprints, brochures, or reports.

- A list of references, with the *name* and *phone number* of the specific person you want the client to talk to (not just the project name).

References

A word about references: They should always be cleared, each time you use them. A leaky roof can change a rave review into a critical disaster overnight. Leave your client an out when you're asking for a recommendation. Word your request so that yes isn't the only possible answer. Then if there's a moment's hesitation, scratch.

Once a potential client called a school district where we had worked. Had he talked to the superintendent we would have received a great reference; instead he talked to a new principal who confused us with the architect and criticized the design. We didn't get the job.

Follow-up

After the presentation, it's up to you to check up on the project. In these situations, no news is bad news. There is a balance between being pesty and being indifferent; you shouldn't be afraid to show continued interest. If you are worried about being too pushy you won't be pushy enough. After the presentation is another occasion for follow-through letters, to thank the client for the opportunity to discuss the project and to express strong enthusiasm for the work ahead. It's good manners.

STAFF SUPPORT

While senior officers must carry the responsibility for bringing in new clients, there are vital functions a staff group can provide: the production of brochures, slides, case histories, proposals, articles for publication, article reprints, press releases, and advertising.

1 *Press releases and articles.* Public relations keeps a company's name in front of the market. It keeps the company from being brand X when the client is draw-

ing up an interview list. There is an opportunity for press exposure when people are promoted, when contracts are awarded, or when the company has developed a new and impressive procedure.

Articles by company leaders are good selling tools, both in the original publication and later as reprints used as promotional literature. They give the company an intellectual base and demonstrate an interest in new developments in the industry. The problems are (1) potential authors get too close to their subject and can't see how impressive their work sounds to someone outside the field, and (2) few construction managers write well. Motivation and encouragement are the answers to the first problem; good professional editors will alleviate the second.

2 *Graphics and slides.* Selling is communication. Pictures and diagrams back up words and allow you to communicate more in less time. Imagine trying to explain a building to a contractor without drawings. Graphics are essential for presentations and can be assembled or developed for each individual project. We have a master slide file that is helpful, but I keep my own file, and so do the others who sell effectively.

3 *Brochures.* All too often brochures are ego trips for company executives, tributes to the company and its works, usually unrelated to the project at hand. But there are brochures that are effective. A brief, general description of the company, its services, experience, and office locations and a list of its well-known clients are useful as an introduction. A more elaborate brochure can be assembled from modular, graphically consistent promotional resource material on file, tailored for a specific client and describing only services and case histories relevant to the project.

4   *Advertising.* Two kinds of advertising are open to construction management companies. One is institutional advertising; its purpose is to establish name recognition. An example is the huge billboard alongside the freeway that reads "Company X welcomes you to Houston." The second kind tries to make a sale by promising a benefit to a buyer. The first can be another ego trip for management, but the second is good business.

We haven't had much experience with advertising yet, but what we have done has been directed at getting jobs, not at setting an institutional image.

We've learned that screening advertising responses is difficult. Our first ad produced about eighty curiosity seekers and no prospects. But we'll continue to advertise, because we have obtained work through our subsequent ads. The trick is to know who the clients will be, decide what to tell them, and figure out how to get them to read it and believe it.

A lot of ads exist, however, because the ad agencies appealed to somebody's self-image—presenting the president's face, for example, or the company's hotshot projects rather than the buyer benefits.

5   *Coordinating direct promotion.* Any company with a number of officers, branch offices, affiliate companies, and joint venture partners involved in direct sales needs a capable officer coordinating these efforts. Otherwise opportunities slip away or are mishandled. To a large company with several divisions, lack of coordination means a real danger of meeting one another at the same interview. It's happened before!

It's essential to have reporting procedures to stay on top of sales efforts. That's true within one company and also among its affiliate companies. The coordinating officers also have to be heavyweight enough to get the attention of the top officers of the company and develop good relations with the development people within the affiliates.

6 *Promotional resource materials.* Adaptable building blocks for brochures, proposals, presentations, and speeches are important. These include items such as article reprints, slides, descriptions of services, rationalizations for the construction management idea, and old proposals that can be used as a basis for new ones. Word processors make tailoring the material to a specific job a lot easier, but they also make it easier to throw in boilerplate.

7 *Management and production of proposals.* Selling a job can require as much specialization and teamwork as the design and construction process. The concepts within the proposal must be tailored to fit the job by the person selling it. If you give a potential client a standard proposal, you'll get a standard reaction: "No thanks."

After the concepts are outlined and the major issues defined, a staff with writing skills can provide writing and editorial support, using building blocks from other proposals, and they can manage the proposal's production.

Writing Proposals

Most proposals have a stuffy cover letter, a boring scope of services, a pretentious description of the company, and a monotonous listing of project experience. Take pity on the client. It would be impossible to evaluate proposals from five different companies if reading the first one put you to sleep. And while a proposal for construction management services will never be a spellbinding literary work, a lot can be done to make it more interesting and intelligible.

The whole story should be told in the cover letter, introduction, foreword, or summary. To be included:

1 *Why yours in the best firm to select.* Use specifics like "We have specialized in the construction management of schools. It's 60% of our practice and includes 80 projects and $300 million of construction." Stuffy generalities such as "We have a proven body of experience in construction of schools with a dedicated team of specialists" are as meaningless and empty here as they are in the presentation. To sound convincing, you must understand the project and your own strengths, especially in comparison with the competition's. Again, it's very tempting to overestimate or exaggerate your talents, but it's sure embarrassing to get caught.

2 *Why you want the job,* if it includes a benefit to your client. "Your project, if properly managed, will have obvious national prestige, which will bring fame to both of us."

3 *What you are going to do,* in specific terms. On one job, we promised the client that we would set up an office in his city. In order to make that soak in, we dummied up a space in our office in Houston to make it resemble the "war room" we were proposing, and had it photographed to show the client what we had in mind. He understood; we got the job.

A summary, always at the front, should convey 98 percent of the message using 2 percent of the words so a busy executive can get the message without falling asleep and so the person who actually reads the whole proposal has a framework of understanding upon moving into the full version.

It's hard to get a comprehensive understanding of a company from the standard list of projects that is always included in proposals. The best way to describe a company is briefly, succinctly, in terms that are important to the client. Here is one I like.

Our company was founded in 1971 by architects and engineers who focused their attention on construction. Because of this background we understand design as well as construction and are particularly qualified to manage the whole project.

We are leaders in the development and application of modern management tools in the construction industry. We use advanced systems of communications, documentation, and information processing. Computer technology developed for several large international projects is routinely applied to all of our work.

We have become widely experienced in the practical realities of construction in the field, and we will guarantee costs and provide bonds in appropriate cases. We spend considerable time staying abreast of labor and material costs. While we are licensed as general contractors in some states, our capacities are broader than those of a typical general contractor.

This passage makes it very clear that we are not architects or contractors and that we have systems and international experience. But it may not be appropriate for the next project, which might be an art museum in Des Moines for a client with a top priority of involving local contractors.

One of our officers wrote a lead-in that is appropriate for any project that has cost savings as a major issue.

Hiring us as your construction manager will cost you $_____ . That's less than _____ percent of the likely total project cost. And by hiring us, you can expect to save 8 to 10 percent beyond our fee. Here's why. . . .

Not only can we save you money, but we can save you time and relieve you of many of the administrative headaches that too often characterize construction projects. As your construction manager, we'll bring control of the project to you. Here's how. . . .

Short proposals are almost always better proposals. It's hard to be brief, but your clients will appreciate it. The U.S. Treasury Department requested that the proposal for the Ministry of Finance Information Center in Saudi Arabia be limited to twenty pages. We did it in nineteen, and it was one of the best proposals we ever put together. We also got the job.

Simple words, graphics, and a distinguished cover letter are the essential components to a good proposal. Most of the time you have to force yourself to be original and fresh, using good material only when it applies. The important parts of a proposal are the sections on (1) services, (2) qualifications, and (3) price. The rest is boilerplate. The most important thing is not to let the support material smother the communication. Keep the issues up front and the backup where it belongs.

PRICING THE JOB AND NEGOTIATING THE FEE

Our third job was competitively bid, and we have bid work ever since. I hope we always will; it forces a company to keep its competitive edge. Most clients want competition, and I don't agree that professionals should be above negotiating fees. The danger lies in the cost of bidding a project that goes automatically to the low bidder because of a vague scope of work or because of competition from incompetent and irresponsible firms. Avoid those projects.

Bidding work requires the thoroughly objective judgment of a group of people familiar with what the project will require and accurate cost information. Unfortunately these people usually bring passionate, emotional influences with them that have nothing to do with determining the right price. Some of the influences we watch out for when we're putting together a bid include price *increases* based on:

- The number of people deciding the scope of services

- The number of joint venture partners

- The number of times the operating staff is asked how much it will need to do the work

and price *decreases* based on:

- The insecurity of the officer selling the job or the length of time since that officer's last sale

- Our conviction that the project is an essential one to our growth

- Our affection for the potential client

We also watch out for common stories that we tell each other too often to rationalize a low fee.

- "If we do this job well it will lead to other work." (That's true of most jobs.)

- "This will be a monument to our ability and creativity." (You won't make a profit from building your own monuments.)

- "We should do this without profit, for the experience." (You get experience from all jobs.)

- "We should fund the development of these new capabilities from profits." (You develop new capabilities on every job.)

We use other stories to convince each other that we should increase our bid:

- "For all this trouble, we deserve more than that." (Trouble can't be billed to the client.)

- "I know he hasn't asked for it, but the client is really going to need our pet services here and there." (You shouldn't be building in special services at this point; the client is calling the shots.)

- "There are a lot of unknowns in this job that we'd better cover for." (There are unknowns in every job, but they'd better not stay unknowns for long.)

The bid team members should learn not to play these old tapes to each other. Teamwork helps when analyzing costs, but the final price, I believe, should be figured with the fewest high-level people possible. There's only one philosophy in pricing work: Bid the highest number that will get the job. If you don't think that will give you the profit you want and support a good job, forget the effort.

Not many construction management projects are straight competitive-bid, but more and more will be in the future. The competition is going to be fierce. One way to avoid pricing yourself too high is by omitting the company's standard services if the client hasn't asked for them, leaving out the pet tricks. You can identify them as optional extras in the fee proposal if appropriate.

WINNING AND LOSING

When you lose, it's important to find out why. It helps you to be better next time, and believe it or not, being a good loser can eventually help bring in work. Any impression you make by being a good sport and by showing high morale and confidence will stick, so that your lost client may remember you upon hearing that someone is in the market for a construction manager.

There is a standard set of good-loser letters, such as "You hired a good firm" (if that's true) and "Thanks for interviewing us." And if you know your competitors, you can write and congratulate them; you may see them on a selection board sometime. You are going to be in business for a long time—so is the client you just lost, and so is the competition. An acquaintance with one of our biggest competitors was on the selection board on an international U.S. Treasury job. I later heard he pulled hard for us. Diplomacy goes a long way.

And now for the best part: winning. It's easy to let down after a hard-earned win. But the first few weeks of a project are the most important. It's essential to get the company's attention on the new job, to get the job off and running. We've taken weeks to get a job started only to wish forlornly for just a few more days to make the deadline at the end. There's a story about the wise fellow who ran all out the last block and still missed the bus. A bystander remarked that he should have run harder. The runner panted, "No, I should have started sooner and walked."

All through a project, there is a reputation to protect. Winning is not the end, it's the beginning.

2

PROJECT-DELIVERY STRATEGIES

The construction industry is changing: projects are larger, building systems are more specialized, and computers and communication techniques have changed management techniques fundamentally. The project-delivery process—getting a project designed and built for the owner—is changing too. We use more technology in the management process now, more consultants and specialists are involved, and clients can choose from more ways to contract for more services to suit their own situations. Construction management, in the beginning, added a new dimension to a construction project's organization; now it is constantly adjusting its services to respond to new needs. With imagination, creativity, and good teamwork, project teams can adapt both their relationships and their contracts to each project's needs. Architects, engineers, and construction managers have learned that they can be as creative about the *process* as about the *product*.

INFLUENCES ON PROJECT-DELIVERY STRATEGY

Both obvious and not so obvious conditions influence the way a project is delivered. Too often we develop fixed notions of how we should serve clients, categorizing all clients as one group with one set of needs. Or worse yet, we develop a professional image of how we should do our job. This condition ignores the fact that developers, institutions, industry, and government all go about design and construction in different ways—for good reasons.

Our own company, in its early years, worked extensively for institutional clients. These clients were often groups—a school board, an administration, and a faculty. They usually had the construction money in the bank from a bond sale. They wanted to be extensively involved in the programming and design process and often wanted a unique and original design. The design would be carefully considered by all, and everyone had to have his or her say. The design had to be negotiated with several people with several interests. Function, aesthetics, and performance were values often placed above economy. These clients were also timid about starting construction before all design decisions were made and until they had a fixed price from bonded contractors to build the project. They were often in a hurry, but as a group, these clients were not prone to take risks, and the notion of overlapping design and construction made them uncomfortable.

As we worked for these early clients we developed a process that would work well for their organizational style. It included extensive conversations to learn the specific needs, prejudices, and ambitions of our clients. Concepts from these conversations that would shape the design were diagramed, recorded, and reviewed. Spaces required for the project were diagramed. Reports were written and reviewed. Then the design team was moved to the site to produce the design with the client looking on. The final design was carefully considered and deliberated. It was also time-consuming and costly. But the institutional client had the money in the bank and *knew* the project was going to be built and therefore didn't mind paying a front-end design fee.

Contrast these needs and pressures with those of a commercial office-building developer. This client probably works as an individual, not with a board. The developer may take out an option to buy a site for 1 percent of the land cost; then it's necessary to find a tenant, obtain permanent and interim financing, and pin down the lease, the design, and the construction cost.

Often none of these things can be done without the others. The developer can't close on the land or the lease without financing. The financing requires getting the lease or the construction price pinned down. And nothing can be done without a design—which also has to be financed. So the developer operates out of pocket with risk money, which will be lost if the project doesn't go ahead—and most don't, as the developer knows only too well.

The glue that sticks this house of cards together is the developer's credibility. Obviously, a 3-month design process won't do—what's needed is an architect who knows good office-building design and can give some kind of picture by Friday, and a contractor or a construction manager who will put a price on the design without working drawings and specs. All for little or no cost. After the package gets put together (often the contracts for the land, the leases, interim and permanent financing, design, and construction are signed in one sitting) the developer can reconsider the design. But not for long—and since there already is a construction price based on sketchy drawings and since this sort of entrepreneur tends to be comfortable with a little risk, the developer will probably start construction long before design is complete.

In its early years, CM Inc., with the processes we had developed for institutional clients, simply couldn't shift gears for the developers' process. We felt they were asking us to be unprofessional, supplying a design and a price without adequate deliberation. Consequently, we didn't work for many. It wasn't until later, with the flexibility that international practice demands, that we learned to adapt our processes to the uniqueness of each client.

For every project, you must take into account the client firm's project objectives, the structure of its organization, and the external pressures of its political, social, cultural, and economic environment. A good construction manager can help a client identify the three influences to be considered (see Figure 2-1).

1 *Project objectives.* The three classic design and construction objectives are quality, cost, and time; everybody wants best quality, least cost, shortest time. Unfortunately, while these goals are not always mutually exclusive, trade-offs usually have to be made. Priorities vary. Most clients have tight budgets that actually define the scope of their projects. Others have inflexi-

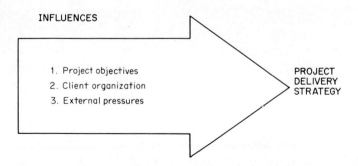

Figure 2-1   Influences on project-delivery strategy.

ble deadlines. Sometimes quality is more important, even though it costs more and takes more time.

Variations in how these objectives are defined compound the difficulty in identifying them. Quality may mean beauty, function, or permanence. Cost may mean initial or long-term prices. Time may mean as soon as possible or by a specific date. Construction managers should help clients determine their definition of terms.

2 *Client's organization.* Clients' attitudes and their staffs' capabilities influence how they go about building a project. Some clients want to be involved in every decision; others want to know only how much the building will cost and when they can move in. A client with a huge internal construction capability is prepared for a multiple-contract approach, which a smaller company might bypass to avoid all the paperwork, the management effort, and the risk.

The client's organization also affects the type of contracts used in the project. A developing country's housing ministry is probably interested in the kind of contracts that require the least amount of supervision and participation from its nonexistent or untrained staff. But a major oil company will probably have a well-trained technical and managerial staff who understand the problems of their business; they'll want to be involved in all the decisions. They will want the time and money savings made possible by a multiple-contract approach, and they'll be able to provide the management that a multiple-contract project-delivery demands.

3 *External pressures.* External pressures—those stemming from sources outside the organization—also influence a client's choice of project-delivery strategies.

An obvious example is public agencies, which are by law answerable to their constituents. They must be demonstrably fair when they contract for services and products; hence their projects usually will be competitively bid.

Other external influences have a less direct, but no less dramatic, effect on the choice of strategies. Sometimes, on large projects, financial guarantee or bonding requirements are so great that special strategies are needed to help contractors bid. It may be necessary to divide the large contract into smaller packages; or, it may be necessary to establish procedures that will encourage several companies to form a large, financially powerful consortium. Because most megaprojects involve imported products, events halfway around the world can act as external influences and affect such things as the availability of fuel and steel or the cost of money. Thus world politics can influence the construction of an industrial plant in Michigan and hence its project delivery.

Furthermore, national goals and policies may affect strategies. In the United States, a project may be divided into many contracts so that small or minority-owned businesses will be able to compete. In the Middle East, where construction labor is imported, the goal is to use capital-intensive building systems to keep labor to a minimum. Other countries want to use labor-intensive building systems to maximize the use of large numbers of unemployed local workers.

These are examples of some obvious, typical external influences. Sometimes these external pressures are openly discussed, sometimes they're not. Watch out for the hidden-agenda pressures that influence clients to select one contracting strategy or team over another. I was told of one client who rejected a multiple-contract approach because he felt it would require too much effort to negotiate the kickbacks, standard practice in his country. One city council wanted to break its project up into little contracts so nonunion contractors would have a better chance of beating the union contractors. These subtle influences you will have to dig for.

CRITICAL DECISIONS

Once they have recognized the organizational, emotional, and political influences they have to deal with, clients face three basic project-delivery decisions. These decisions determine the way the project is structured; they form the framework for the project strategy. The decisions to be made are (1) the *number of contracts to be used* in the project (ranging from one to many); (2) the *criteria to be used* to select the various project participants (by qualifications, by cost, or a combination of the two); and (3) the *type of contracts to be used* with each project participant (ranging from agent to vendor agreements).

With these issues settled, the construction manager (or CM) and the client can determine how the project will be organized, how it will be contracted and paid for, how the team members will relate to each other and the client, and how involved the client will be in the project. The variations and combinations are virtually limitless (see Figure 2-2).

1 *Number of contracts.* A client can buy a project in one contract, as in design-build; in two contracts, as in the traditional process; in multiple construction contracts, as in a typical fast-track–construction management project; or in hundreds of contracts, the

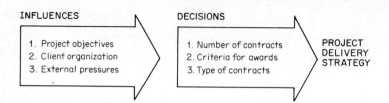

INFLUENCES

1. Project objectives
2. Client organization
3. External pressures

DECISIONS

1. Number of contracts
2. Criteria for awards
3. Type of contracts

PROJECT
DELIVERY
STRATEGY

Figure 2-2 Project-delivery decisions.

client personally buying all materials and hiring all individuals required to do the work (see Figure 2-3).

As contracts increase in number, the potential for economy, speed, flexibility, and control also increases. But more contracts also demand greater management skill, and risks in cost, scheduling, and procurement increase too.

2 *Criteria for award.* Project participants—architect, engineer, construction manager, contractors—can be selected either on the basis of their experience and resources, or on the fee proposals and management plans they submit, or on the basis of price, whether it is a restricted or an open bid. Some clients base their awards on all these criteria.

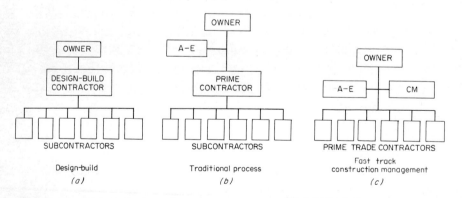

OWNER

OWNER

DESIGN-BUILD
CONTRACTOR

SUBCONTRACTORS

Design-build

(a)

A-E

PRIME
CONTRACTOR

SUBCONTRACTORS

Traditional process

(b)

OWNER

A-E　CM

PRIME TRADE CONTRACTORS

Fast track
construction management

(c)

Figure 2-3 Different ways of buying a project: (*a*) one contract; (*b*) two contracts; (*c*) many contracts.

By experience and resources. Clients often select an agent, someone they expect to represent them professionally, solely on the basis of experience and resources. This is, in fact, the most common way of choosing architects and engineers, who are generally paid a professional fee based on the type and amount of service they provide. A client who wants exceptional quality or proprietary technology may also forgo the more typical bidding process and negotiate directly with a *vendor* solely on the basis of qualifications.

By fee proposal and management plan. Project participants are often asked to submit a detailed plan outlining their projected team organization, their schedules, their strategies, and the fee for their services. So, in addition to qualifications, the client evaluates potential companies on such things as their proposed scope of services, their resources, their management procedures, and their allowances for profit and overhead.

By price. At the other end of the spectrum is selection based on price alone. Cost is a traditional way to contract for both general contractor and subcontractors. But the client often blends in qualification criteria by organizing what is called a *restricted* bid, where contractors are prequalified according to their resources, reputation, or capability of performing the work required and issued an invitation to bid.

This approach is becoming more common in bidding on services as well, as with construction management or architecture-engineering fees. Restricted bids make sense: blue-ribbon contractors, CMs, and A-Es are more likely to respond to a bid invitation if their competition is select. *Open-bid*, on the other hand, can be a terrible waste of time—unless the product being bid is extremely common or its quality specifiable. In these cases, the range of prices can be as much as 200 percent, so it pays to shop around.

Bonding is a means of restricting bidding. Public bidding for construction is not entirely open, because public agencies require bonds—technically speaking, they are using the bonding companies' prequalification criteria.

3 *Contract types.* For each contract to be awarded, a client must decide whether to treat the project participant as an agent or as a vendor. The choice is basically this: A vendor sells a product for a price; an agent acts in the client's interest for a fee. When doing business with a vendor, the client is more interested in the product and its price than in the qualifications of the seller. In dealing with an agent the concern rests primarily with the seller's experience, qualifications, and integrity.

But nothing stops a client from choosing an architectural firm on the basis of qualifications (as an agent) and then buying a design from the firm at a fixed fee (treating it as a vendor). Furthermore, few contracts produce a clear-cut agent or vendor relationship. An architect or contractor whose fee is a percentage of the construction cost, and who influences that cost, is acting as both agent and vendor. So is a contractor who agrees to work for cost plus a fee with a guaranteed maximum price. Many lump-sum (vendor) construction contracts require the contractor to advise the client or the architect if unsound construction methods are used or errors occur, responsibilities that generally fall into the agent category. While a mixed relationship can create a conflict of interest, these types of contracts are common in the industry. You just have to make sure that the contract is clear and that everyone understands its terms.

After investing a great deal of creative thought into analyzing the best way to deliver a project, a construction manager may be thwarted by resistance to change. The construction industry's glacial inertia hinders innovation. It's an uphill fight—most strategies are used because "that's the way it's always been done." Tradition and custom support familiar processes. Sometimes it is better to manage a familiar but awkward process than to make the people you're trying to help uncomfortable and confused with a new approach. Never forget: What's best is what works.

Contract Types: The Choices

Simple projects usually can be handled by simple contracts. But as complexities increase so does the need for other, more responsive contract forms. The more you move toward the agent end of the spectrum, the more variations there are on the simple "for this much work, I'll pay you this amount of money" contract. Each team member's effect on the outcome of the project should be reflected in his or her contractual relationship with the client. Companies should be hired for standard, specific tasks with standard, fixed-fee contracts. Companies with profit and loss responsibility should have contracts that encourage them to save money with bonus incentives.

The range of contract types is basically shown in Figure 2-4.

AGENT   VENDOR

Cost plus	Target price	Guaranteed maximum price	Unit-price – quantity survey	Stipulated sum

Figure 2-4   Types of contracts.

Cost of Work plus a Fee

Cost-plus contracts begin at the agency end of the spectrum. Essentially the contractor is reimbursed for all expenses and is paid a fixed fee for overhead and profit. Where time, flexibility, technology, or quality is of concern to the client, cost-plus contracts offer the greatest advantages. Their drawback is that the client's final cost isn't tied down at the project start. The variations on cost-plus contracts include:

• *Simple cost plus a fee.* The contractor is paid incurred cost plus a fee based on either a lump sum or a percentage of cost. Lump sums allow contractors to provide savings to clients without penalizing themselves. With a percentage of cost, the fee moves up or down with the size of the project. The drawback here is an apparent conflict of interest: The contractor can increase the fee by permitting high costs.

• *Target price plus a fee.* A target price for the project is figured on the basis of the contract documents, performance specifications, standard square footage costs, or unit costs, or a combination of these. The fee is usually fixed. A provision is added to allow the contractor to share in any savings below the target price or to participate in cost overruns.

• *Partial guarantee plus a fee.* Often in cost-plus contracts the contractor guarantees part of the project cost.

Guarantees are commonly given for prepurchased equipment, materials, and subcontracts, and occasionally for labor, which may be subcontracted before construction begins.

• *Cost plus a fee with a guaranteed price.* Contractors can assume responsibility for all costs over a stipulated price. But because they are then accepting risks beyond the amount of their fee, self-preservation dictates that they include a contingency and set as high a maximum as possible. A clause may be added to enable them to share in savings if the final price is less than the guaranteed price.

Unit-Price—Quantity Survey

Quantity surveys are used widely in the United Kingdom and in parts of the Middle East. A quantity surveyor supplies potential contractors with a detailed list of building material quantities (bills of quantities). The contractors then figure and apply unit prices for the installed price of the materials. An advantage of the quantity-survey contract is that contracts can be awarded on the basis of approximate quantities, before drawings and specifications are actually completed, and in situations where quantities are unknown, as with rock excavation.

The bidding or negotiating process is accelerated in the quantity-survey method, since the contractors don't have to estimate quantities of materials from drawings and specifications. The contractor is paid for actual quantities used at the unit price that was specified. If there is substantial error in the survey, the quantity surveyor may be held responsible. A weakness is that a bill of quantities does not exactly account for the ways a contractor incurs costs.

Stipulated Sum

The polar opposite of the cost-plus contract is the stipulated-sum contract. Normally, for stipulated-sum to be totally enforceable, a complete, detailed set of plans and specifications defining the project must be prepared first. Bidding or negotiating follows. The contractor assumes the role of a vendor who agrees to construct the project in accordance with the detailed plan and with all applicable laws and regulations for the fixed sum. Like a speculator on the market who has sold short, the contractor has sold a building not yet bought.

The greatest advantage of stipulated-sum is that the client knows very early what the financial commitment is for the entire project. However, the contractor may execute the contractual obligations with only secondary consideration to quality or schedule. Since any savings directly increase the contractor's profits, this type of agreement requires the client's careful attention to contract compliance.

Another disadvantage with stipulated-sum agreements is that changes can be difficult and costly, as the contractor will likely be reluctant to interrupt the tight production schedule. But the greatest disadvantage with stipulated-sum contracts is the time lost in waiting for construction documents to be finished before the contract is signed and work begun.

PROJECT STRATEGIES

Once the client knows what influences must be considered (the project objectives, the structure of the organization, and the external pressures) in order to make the three critical decisions (how many contracts to let out,

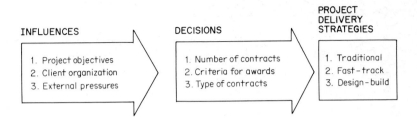

Figure 2-5 Project-strategy options.

how to choose the team, and how to contract and work with the team), it's time to evaluate the project-strategy options (see Figure 2-5). Both client and construction manager must keep in mind that these are typical arrangements and should be considered frameworks only. Standard procedures are constantly changing to accommodate new projects and new clients (see Figure 2-6).

PROJECT STRATEGIES							
Single-point	Design-build	Turnkey	Fast-track multiple-contract	Traditional	O Occasional ● Usual		
O	●	●		O	Simple cost of work + fee	COST OF WORK PLUS A FEE	CONTRACT TYPE (FOR CONSTRUCTION CONTRACTS)
O	●				Target price		
O	●				Partial guarantee		
O	●	O	●		Guaranteed maximum price		
●	●	●	●	●	Unit-price- Quantity Survey		
●	●	●	●	●	Stipulated sum		

Figure 2-6 Project strategies and contract types.

The Traditional Process

A client organization needs a building. The company hires an architect, whom it pays a fee to represent its interests. The architect designs the building, produces the working drawings and specs, has it bid by contractors, and checks construction to ensure that the client company gets what it pays for. The architect is a professional who rents expertise to the client, thus acting as an agent on the client's behalf.

The prime contractor's relationship with the client is different from the architect's. Such contractors are vendors, selling a building, and are usually selected by price rather than by integrity or professionalism, although they may have both. Every dollar they spend cuts into their own profit, so it's in their own best interest to be tight-fisted with quality: their legal responsibility is to provide what is on the plans and specifications (see Figure 2-7).

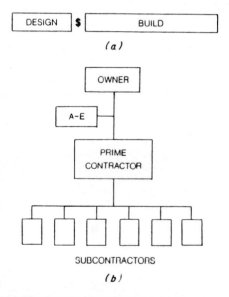

Figure 2-7 Traditional process: (a) Time sequence, left to right. $ indicates bid and award stage. (b) Relationships among parties.

The persuasive arguments for this traditional process are management simplicity and cost security. Getting the design worked out, the working drawings and specifications completely done, and all the decisions made before construction starts will simplify the client's and the architect's management duties. Awarding the bid to one contractor who agrees to deliver the project according to plans and specs for a fixed, bonded price will secure their costs.

So what are the traditional strategy's flaws? It takes too long. And it costs too much.

While the traditional process is prudent in theory (the only financial risk the client takes before getting a bonded total price is the design fee), inflation plays havoc with its brand of security. In a stable economy, projects bid over the budget can be redesigned and rebid. But during inflationary times, the client and the architect have a receding target; even with reduced scope, the project might be rebid at a higher price.

The traditional process also takes so long that often a project has costly changes before construction is even begun. We once did a study of a large university's building program to determine when its buildings would need remodeling. Instead of the usual bell-shaped curve with frequency patterns peaking at about 5 years, the most common point was 6 months *before* initial occupancy. It had taken so long to get the project designed and built that the facilities were outdated before they were occupied.

Another fault with the traditional process is the isolated design phase. Architects generally have little or no experience with actually buying materials, equipment, and labor. The traditional process excludes the people who know the most about construction cost and construction techniques (the contractors) from the design phase, which is when cost and construction problems are built in. After design is complete, nobody wants to change it.

Stipulated-sum or lump-sum competitive bidding is the standard contracting strategy for the traditional process, supposedly because of its economy. But therein lies another superstition, because competitive bidding rarely produces the lowest price. In the last, heated hours of a bid period it is almost impossible for a general contractor to ferret out the lowest bid in each of perhaps a hundred categories of subcontractors and material suppliers. And the low bidder will never have the low subcontractor bid in every category. Single–lump-sum competitive bidding just can't deliver the best overall bid.

While the traditional process is simple to administer and apparently prudent economically, it is neither the fastest nor the most economical project delivery strategy.

Fast-Track–Construction Management

Fast-track strategies came about because the client and the architect realized that a lot of construction could go on before the working drawings and specifications were complete. Things like the cabinet details, the door details, and the hardware specs are inconsequential until construction reaches a detailed stage. Meanwhile, the site can be cleared. When the location of the building on the site is known, grading can begin. And once the geometry of the building is defined, the structure can be ordered.

In fast-track strategies, a client and an architect-engineer (A-E) plan the design process as a series of design decisions progressing from the comprehensive to the more detailed. A portion of the construction follows each major set of decisions, with the team doing business directly with the subcontractors. In this arrangement design and construction are viewed as one continuous process. The overlap can save much time and therefore much money.

With the potential for big savings through fast-track, clients are willing to take some risk. But the management complications entailed by fast-track contracts require more applied management than architects or clients are usually prepared to provide. They demand management of multiple-contract bidding, extremely accurate estimating and scheduling, and coordination of construction contracts in the field. Fast-track's method of overlapping design and construction schedules makes it an ideal candidate for construction management services. In a fast-track construction contract strategy, the construction expert acts as the client's agent, while contractors typically use vendor contracts (see Figure 2-8).

Delivery time is shortened by arranging the process so that more people can work simultaneously. Design and working drawings are overlapped with construction activities, and construction in the field is overlapped with the manufacture of components and equipment. If all these things are managed well, fast-track comes off like a beautifully choreographed ballet. If not, problems are compounded until it is bad burlesque. Good construction management is great; bad construction management is terrible.

It was when fast-track came into general use (around 1970) that construction management emerged as a profession. The administrative aspects of a construction project had become a full-time job. So a construction manager (CM) was added to the organizational structure to act as an owner's representative in conceiving and implementing a project strategy.

With fast-track–construction management, general contractors with their overhead and profit are usually

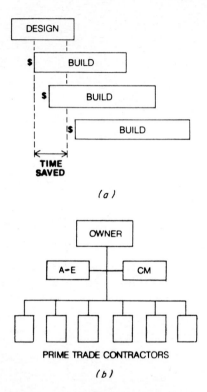

Figure 2-8 Fast-track–construction management strategy: (*a*) Time sequence, left to right. $ indicates bid and award stage. (*b*) Relationships among parties.

eliminated, although the construction manager may actually act as a contractor on most other jobs and the CM fee might equal the overhead and profit of a general contractor. The general contractor's role is played by the construction manager. But the construction manager expands that role by advising on construction, schedules, and costs from the start of design.

Another difference between a general contractor and a CM: Throughout the world most public laws require that government agencies buy by competitive bid. There are two simple reasons: Bidding theoretically gives everyone an equal shot at doing business on public funds, and the belief is that the lowest bid will spend the fewest tax dollars. A general contractor is usually chosen by low bid and not necessarily by past performance. But because a construction manager sells *services* instead of *products*, a public client can choose a construction manager on the basis of qualifications rather than on price alone.

A general contractor subcontracts most of the construction to specialty-trade contractors. Actually, some contractors simply provide the bond and the overall coordination and subcontract all the work. But as an agent, the construction manager can contract directly with these subcontractors on the client's behalf, bidding or negotiating each contract in sequence as the contract demands. Dealing directly with the organizations that furnish the labor and materials unearths economies, opportunities for additional cost and time savings, and the lowest price for each contractor or supplier. Thus the construction industry's increasing specialization invites construction management. Furthermore, the construction manager is available to advise the owner and the A-E on construction cost and technology during the design phase.

One major weakness is inherent in fast-track–construction management arrangements. By its very nature, fast-track makes it difficult to fix or guarantee a price before work begins. Even when the early stages of the project, such as site work and foundations, are under contract, there may be no assurance that the rest of the contracts will come in within the client's budget. There are two common solutions:

• *Guaranteed maximum price* (GMP). The construction manager guarantees the client that project cost will not exceed x dollars and pledges to pay any overrun. Guaranteed-price sounds very attractive to a client, but it has a hitch in fast-track schedules—again by definition. Construction is begun without complete working drawings and specs. The construction manager is guaranteeing a vague scope of work. Because of this uncertainty, a GMP can mean downstream arguments over exactly *what* the construction manager guaranteed to build for the maximum price.

If the client is dealing with responsible people, the GMP process works very well. But it's the construction manager's desire to maintain a good reputation that makes this arrangement successful—not a contract.

• *The agent–construction manager.* In this solution, construction managers become the clients' agents and work only in their behalf. They assure their clients that their expertise will keep a project within its budget. As drawings and specifications are completed for each phase of the work, the contracts are systematically awarded, often by competitive bid.

But if the construction manager's cost estimates for downstream contracts are too low when construction begins, the client will be in trouble. And even the most advanced, sophisticated estimating can be wrong. A management *strategy* is what minimizes risk for the client and makes these arrangements successful.

In some cases, agent–construction managers will set up a project contingency and establish some alternatives on each of the bid packages. They may bid some equipment and products with the early construction contracts to get the prices tied down; they may then delay starting construction until 50 percent of the cost is known. With the contingency, the alternatives, and good estimates, a

CM can be sure that the project will be brought in under the budget.

Design-Build Contracts

Design-build contracts are based on the concept of integrating design and construction as one process within a single contract (see Figure 2-9).

The rationale for design-build is that the bodies of expertise in design and construction are so closely related that it is inefficient to hire an A-E and then wait to hire a contractor until design is complete. The integration of the two fields results in improvements in cost, time, and construction technology. And with only one organization, the client can figure on having centralized knowl-

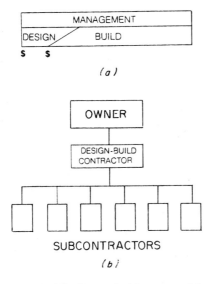

Figure 2-9 Design-build contract: (*a*) Time sequence, left to right. $ indicates bid and award stage. (*b*) Relationships among parties.

edge of both design and construction, plus undivided responsibility.

Sometimes design-build contractors don't have in-house design capabilities. To design the building, they simply hire architects and engineers as they would hire other subcontractors. The client reviews designs submitted by the design-build firm but is not generally involved in their development after the initial stages. A-Es working under this arrangement usually can't obtain errors and omissions insurance, because their client is a contractor, not the owner, and the insurance companies figure that the contractor is a vendor rather than a professional agent.

The world's biggest construction organizations are design-build companies, so the concept obviously works. But the various ways to structure design-build contracts and processes have different applications. Here are some of them.

- *Lump-sum design-build*. In this arrangement a design-build contractor agrees to provide some front-end design services for a client for a full professional fee, for a loss-leader fee, or for nothing, figuring that the eventual contract will be sufficient compensation. A final lump-sum price may be based on performance specs, a general written description of what the client wants, or scope design drawings. If the initial design and cost proposals are not accepted by the client, the agreement is terminated and the entire process must begin again. If accepted, the project moves ahead.

Lump-sum design-build contracts are often used for light industrial facilities or for housing projects in developing countries—projects where a breakdown of what is to be built is simple and easy to formulate. A housing project of 1000 units, for example, can be broken down into perhaps only five floor plans repeated 200 times. Lump-sum design-build contracts offer speed and low cost in these cases. They are simple to administer, since there is only one contract to manage.

However, this type of contract has its drawbacks. Since the design-build contractor prepares all plans and specs, the client has little control or flexibility after signing the contract. Laws and traditions usually prevent design-build contracts if public funds are involved. Also, it may be difficult to make objective price and quality evaluations among lump-sum design-build organizations because of the radical differences between the systems and products they offer.

Perhaps the most troubling aspect of this process is the cost risk in the front-end design phase for either the contractor or the owner. The design-build company doesn't want to do the design on speculation, because the client may not go ahead with them or the project. Clients won't want to pay the fee for design without knowing what they will be getting and what it will cost.

Other flaws: If selection is based on price alone, quality may suffer; and since the lump-sum contract is often signed on skimpy drawings, a client may end up with something entirely different from what was expected. The client purchases a complete package of services and products and therefore cannot choose the best elements from different companies and combine them at will. And if the initial design proposal is rejected as a whole by the client, then the time spent up to that point has achieved nothing.

• *Cost-reimbursable design-build.* In this arrangement, the prime contractor is usually reimbursed for the cost of all the trade contracts, which the client has the right to approve. The project is broken up into bid packages, and subcontractors are selected to perform the tasks they do best. A basic fee is set for the design-build contractor, sometimes with incentives and a target cost or GMP. There is complete disclosure of the costs to the design-build contractor, who acts as the client's agent.

Cost-reimbursable design-build contracts are often used in high-tech or process projects, such as power or petrochemical plants, where the client is an organization that understands both design and construction and feels competent to manage such a demanding contract. Clients like this usually award cost-reimbursable design-build contracts on the cumulative basis of a firm's qualifications, performance, fee, and management plan. High quality can be obtained with this contract, and the client has extensive control and flexibility throughout the process.

But these contracts are difficult to administer. The client must monitor the project-delivery process and audit expenditures. Public bidding laws aren't written with design-build in mind and may make the process illegal for public organizations. Furthermore, the absence of a fixed price up front may trouble some clients, and the cost-reimbursable aspect may lower the contractor's motivation to save money.

• *Design-bid-build*. This contracting strategy is used primarily in the public sector. A design-build contractor is usually considered a vendor, and competitive-bidding laws usually prevent the selection of a vendor by negotiation. To obtain the benefits of design-build, some public clients prepare the descriptions of the project they want, sometimes with performance specs or preliminary design drawings prepared by an outside consultant or the client's own staff—in effect roughing out the design of the project. Then these drawings are bid by design-build contractors, who have a degree of latitude in the

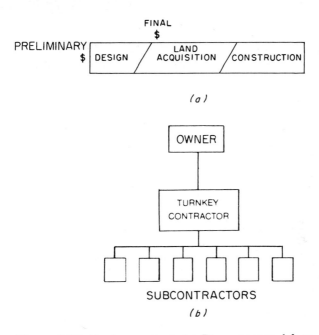

Figure 2-10 Turnkey contract: (*a*) Time sequence, left to right. $ indicates bid and award stage. (*b*) Relationships among parties.

final, detailed development and in execution of the preliminary design. The selection is usually made on the basis of price, but it may include some evaluation of the detailed design.

- *Turnkey.* "Turnkey" is a term that is often used interchangeably with the various design-build approaches (see Figure 2-10). But if there is a difference, it is in the fact that turnkey contracts may go beyond design and construction and may include other functions, such as site acquisition, financing, start-up, operations and maintenance, and staff training. Often clients who want minimum involvement use this contract.

- *Single-Point.* Single-point contracting arrangements are those that simply combine the design and construction management services into one contract, with the client holding all construction contracts directly. They are often called A-E–CM or *professional* design-build. The fundamental difference between single-point and conventional design-build contracts is that in single-point the construction contracts are with the owner (see Figure 2-11).

The A-E–CM contract is usually some version of a professional fee arrangement, while the construction contracts usually are stipulated-sum or unit-price. Contracts for cost of work plus fee are used occasionally for the contractors. And a guaranteed maximum price may be given by the A-E–CM.

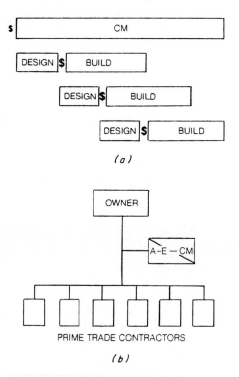

Figure 2-11 Single-point contract: (*a*) Time sequence, left to right. $ indicates bid and award stage. (*b*) Relationships among parties.

Integrated A-E–CM contracts foster coordination and efficiency in design and construction management. The process offers quality, speed, and low cost. The client can award construction contracts by competitive bid, as public bidding laws commonly require.

Dividing the project into manageable parcels simplifies obtaining financial guarantees and bonding. It is a way the public sector may use the advantages of integrated design and construction contracts. And the single-point process simplifies the client's administrative requirements, because one organization can be held responsible for the final result.

The single-point process has its weaknesses too. Some clients object to the joining of forces by the architect, the engineer, and the construction manager. They want the independent voices of each to serve as a check-and-balance system.

Variations on the Themes

The previous discussion lists the most classic strategies for project delivery, but almost every project combines and modifies these strategies. Here are some variations:

• *Fast-track–single-contract*. Hiring a reputable local contractor at the same time as the architect is an adaptation of the traditional approach commonly used in the private sector to achieve the benefits of overlapping design and construction. Since construction is started before design is complete, a stipulated-sum contract is impractical. (See Figure 2-12.)

The usual contract is cost-plus with a guaranteed maximum price, although any type of cost-plus contract or unit-price contract can be used. During construction,

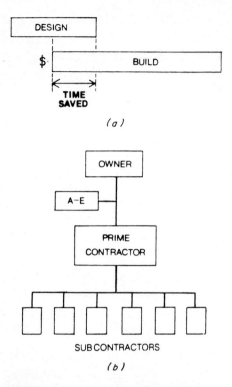

Figure 2-12 The fast-track—single-contract approach: (*a*) Time sequence, left to right. $ indicates bid and award stage. (*b*) Relationships among parties.

the contract may be renegotiated into a lump-sum contract.

The single-contract variation has distinct advantages. The overlap of design and construction saves time and usually money. The contractor provides cost and technical advice in the design phase, and since contractors in this case are selected more by qualifications than by price, project quality is often improved.

The fast-track–single-contract arrangement also has disadvantages. Public clients usually can't use the process, since the overall construction contract can't be competitively bid. The contractor's guaranteed maximum price will normally be given on incomplete plans and specs, which could mean conflict over just what was promised to the client for the stated price.

- *Staged design and construction.* Some private-sector clients, such as universities, housing developments, or resort communities, have building programs that comprise several individual projects. Often the schedule for all the individual projects is not known when the program begins. For example, in a resort community the rate of lot sales may dictate the rate of the construction of the golf course, the marina, the yacht club, the clubhouse, the roads, and the utilities.

Therefore, when the contractor is brought on board to begin work, there are still subsequent contracts to be awarded. The possibility of winning those contracts is an incentive to the contractor. A contractor who keeps on doing a good job can expect to continue to receive new contracts. (See Figure 2-13.)

Any type of contract form can be used with staged design and construction, but the administrative task with this strategy is complex.

- *Sprint-start or premobilization.* On large projects in areas lacking a highly developed and specialized construction infrastructure (as in sparsely populated regions in the United States or in developing countries), a contractor must provide resources that would be taken for granted in a developed or urban area.

The contractor working in an American city has full labor and materials resources available; subcontractors and material companies are only a phone call away. In remote areas contractors must arrange for and supply their own labor, materials, and housing, and all of the

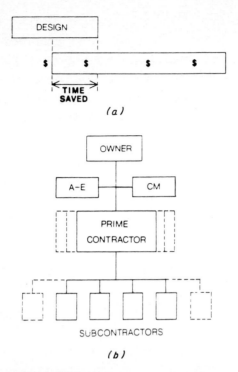

Figure 2-13 Staged design and construction: (a) Time sequence, left to right. $ indicates bid and award stage. (b) Relationships among parties.

logistics of the supply business, including inland transport, inspection, and materials tracking. They may have to build their own concrete plants. The multiple prime trade contractor process won't work in these situations, because the trade contractors just aren't there. The same labor force that digs the foundation mops the roof.

Sprint-start helps save time in this environment. Often on a large project in a developing country or an isolated location, the first 6 to 9 months of the construction contract are devoted to the mobilization phase. Labor camps, precast factories, or batch plants must be built.

Materials and equipment must be purchased, fabricated, and shipped.

Purchasing these mobilization contracts during the design phase, before the award of the general construction contract, saves time. The contracts can be assigned to the contractor after the final design is complete. (See Figure 2-14).

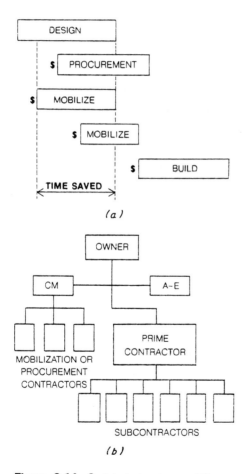

(a)

(b)

Figure 2-14 Sprint-start, or premobilization: (*a*) Time sequence, left to right. $ indicates bid and award stage. (*b*) Relationships among parties.

Usually the mobilization and construction contracts are either competitively bid stipulated-sum, or unit-price–quantity-survey contracts.

• *Multiple contracts with traditional scheduling.* Often a construction manager is involved in projects where there is no overlapping of design and construction. The time saved by fast-track is lost, and contractors may resent the delay between contract bid and award. However, the corresponding advantage is that no construction is begun until the total cost of the project is known. (See Figure 2-15.)

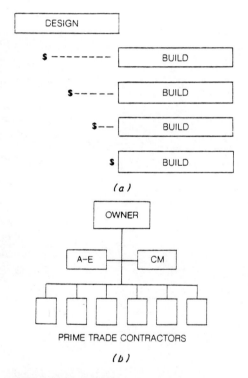

Figure 2-15 Multiple contracts with traditional scheduling: (*a*) Time sequence, left to right. $ indicates bid and award stage. (*b*) Relationships among parties.

All the other advantages of construction management are implemented—such as sequential purchasing of contracts, on-course corrections and cost-control assurance, advice and recommendations on construction technology to the design group, and good control and flexibility in the field.

• *Construction consulting.* The term "construction management" is sometimes used to describe forms of construction consulting services other than the construction management contract strategy.

A construction management organization can provide consulting services. Some clients use a construction manager to represent them in the traditional process when a design-build or a turnkey contract is used. In these instances, the construction manager is a consultant rather than an active member of the project team.

You can see that there isn't just one superior project-delivery method. Too many individual factors have to be considered, and every project is unique. The industry isn't turning to design-build as the ultimate solution, or to turnkey—although when these approaches were first developed that was what we thought would happen. Many people are still very successful using the traditional approach on all of their projects.

The point is that developing the best delivery strategy is a creative process. It's the construction manager's responsibility to know the options and to be able to evaluate them in light of a project's characteristics. Good planning at this stage will save thousands of headaches later on.

3

SAVING
TIME
AND
MONEY
ON
CONSTRUCTION
PROJECTS

In construction management companies—those established and operated for that sole purpose—the effort is focused more on management than on construction. Construction managers are not in the fabrication business; their product is information. A construction manager's primary responsibility is analyzing project-delivery alternatives, establishing project-delivery strategies, communicating them to the people who provide design and construction services, and managing them through to their completion.

Construction management is nothing more than good sense. The ideas behind this business are simple, and there is no mystery to good management. Good construction management is simply staying on top of the thousands of details involved in project delivery.

But here's the catch, here's why so many projects have difficulty: Most smart people don't like detail. They want to deal with concepts and leave the details to the support people. That won't work in construction management. It demands people smart enough to handle both concepts *and* details. Eventually all those little details produce a large project.

Recently I reviewed a cost analysis of construction management and the traditional construction process. The statistics indicated that construction management projects were marginally less expensive than those constructed under the traditional process, although there were extreme variations, both high and low, for the CM projects figured into the average. The analysis missed the whole point. Construction management increases control, which makes major time and cost savings over the traditional process possible. But if that control isn't exercised, the results are worse, not better. Good construction management is great; bad construction management is awful. Averaging the two is meaningless.

The following principles outline ways to exercise control over a construction project. If these fundamentals are observed, you will save time and money on your project; if they are energetically applied, you can expect spectacular results.

PROJECT MANAGEMENT

A construction manager's first job is human engineering: turning a group of clients, architects, engineers, and contractors—perhaps strangers at the start—into a cohesive team that will create a unique, complex product. The way to start is with *planning*, defining the project goals, developing the strategy, and establishing team communications; *organizing*, structuring and staffing the team, and coordinating the construction management staff with that of the client and the other consultants and contractors; and *monitoring*, establishing a regular reporting system for the project team.

Planning

1 *Define project goals.* Hundreds of people make millions of decisions in the course of any one construction project. Some are made in boardrooms, some on site, some on the drawing board. Most of the people making the decisions see only the part of the project that involves them—whether it's the schedule, the schematics, the concrete purchase order, or the accounting reports. A big picture, outlined by a clear, concise summary of the project goals, helps the periodically involved people make better decisions.

Left to themselves, most professionals naturally tend to pursue their own interests rather than the project's. An architect may become intent on design; a construction manager may concentrate on the issues of cost and time. A clear statement of the project's goals consolidates the various members of the team by bringing the real target of their efforts into focus.

When developing a set of project goals, remember that the only meaningful goals are those that are easily measured and quantified. Platitudes are a waste of time—everybody wants economy, speed, and quality. Their order of priority is important, as well as their relationship to the specifics of a particular project. What else matters? Maintenance costs? Energy use? Image? Environment?

It's also important to record the goals and call the project team's attention to them periodically. We developed a form (shown in Figure 3-1) for just this

PROJECT GOALS

PROJECT   INTERCONTINENTAL HOTEL
(Demo)

DATE   6 OCTOBER 1980

GENERAL STATEMENT

To design and manage the construction of a 250-room hotel to be built in Central City, U.S.A. The project shall include public areas consisting of restaurant facilities, shops, a lounge, a ballroom, recreational facilities, and associated hotel service areas. Approximate building area of the project is to be 164,000 square feet.

COST

Construction cost should be competitive with other hotels of similar quality recently built in Central City. A cost of $50,000 to $53,000 per room is to be targeted.

TIME

Construction is to begin in early 1980. The project will be completed approximately 12 months after construction begins.

QUALITY

The hotel is to be of above-average quality, competitive in its finishes with other hotels of its caliber.

Figure 3-1 Project goals.

purpose, which we keep at the front of our project manual as a foreword to the detail that follows.

2 *Create a project strategy.* A project strategy is the plan of attack on the work required to complete a construction project. It is the result of the initial team sessions, which we dedicate to identifying the characteristics and needs of a project and possible alternatives to respond to these needs. It's a plan, an approach, an outline of how the project will eventually come together. (See Figure 3-2.)

The project strategy should contain a definition of the client's approval process, of the basic bid packages, of the cost to be under contract before construction starts, and of the required government approvals. The financial risks inherent in the overlap of design and construction should be identified at this point, along with the management procedure necessary to control that risk.

In creating a project strategy, though, a construction manager must remember that this part of the job is not purely technical, based on computer runs and calculated costs. People bring attitudes to their construction projects, and it's a CM's responsibility to incorporate those attitudes into the project-delivery strategy. It's an old maxim: People do best what they *want* to do, and clients will be much more responsive to your concepts if you take their feelings into consideration. Respect the human factor in planning a strategy.

3 *Document procedures.* Every project is different and requires a little modification of the standard routing and decision-making procedures. The project team and the client should agree on how their organization will be set up and operated. Decision makers should

PROJECT STRATEGY	PROJECT	UNIVERSITY
	DATE	JUNE 1980

To facilitate an accelerated, phased design and construction schedule, the project has been organized into seven major contract areas of responsibility.

1   Central Services Unit/Disposal Services Unit

    Total central services and disposal services for the entire campus complex, including all necessary utility infrastructure for the proposed University Medical Center.

2   Site Improvements

    All required site development: grading, road work, site irrigation, landscaping, etc.

3   Academic Areas – Phase I

    Includes office, classroom, and light and heavy laboratory spaces.

4   Academic Areas – Phase II

    Includes office classroom, and light and heavy laboratory spaces.

5   Campus Spine Network

    Includes both primary and secondary spine networks, including utility tunnels and computerized people-mover facilities.

6   Central Zone Facilities – Phase I

    Includes chapel, library, and hall.

7   Central Zone Facilities – Phase II

    Includes student center, administration building, and athletic facilities.

At this time, each of the above areas represents singular contractual responsibility. As design progresses and specific materials are selected for the various buildings and support facilities, this strategy will be investigated further. It may be necessary at that time to further define the strategy into additional or fewer contract areas.

Figure 3-2   Project strategy.

be identified, the approval process described, and steps to getting bills presented named.

The construction manager should stay flexible in this respect. The client who hasn't had much construction experience will need help creating the appropriate procedures. But clients who have gone through many building programs probably have their own systems set up. And sometimes, though it's painful to admit, they're better. So on every project you must make an objective judgment, and if it makes sense, adapt to the client's procedures, learning from them in the process. It's stupid to get stuck on "the company way" or let ego get in the way of performance.

Back in 1968 we were hired by the New York State University Construction Fund to study ways to accelerate and improve control on design and construction. We talked to many major builders around the country and put their best ideas into a report we titled "Fast Track." The report spelled out procedures for phased design and construction, construction management, and systems building that have since become standard in the industry. We used these concepts as the foundation of CM Inc.

Everybody claims to have invented fast-track, and those claims are probably true. Not one idea in the report was original with us—we only put a name to the process. But fast-track helped CM Inc. build a reputation for using progressive techniques, and it's unstated company policy to pick brains relentlessly. I shudder when I hear statements like "That's not the way we do it."

4   *Establish communication.* Good project management is often nothing more than doing simple things on time. For the most part, that depends on com-

CM

PROJECT DIRECTORY	PROJECT	DEMONSTRATION PROJECT
		CENTRAL CITY, OHIO
	DATE	15 APRIL 1980

OWNER'S REPRESENTATIVE

Mr. Robert Tennant, Tennant Development
7575 S. Alhambra Avenue
Central City, Ohio 43568
Office: 419/173-9087 Home: 419/555-9008

A/E REPRESENTATIVE

Mr. Jordan Ireland, Ireland/Pratt/Theriot
741 Afton
Central City, Ohio 43568
Office: 419/170-3223 Home: 419/174-9853

CM PROJECT MANAGER

Jim Drayton
11211 Heron Way
Central City, Ohio 43568
Home: 449/177-9844

NAME, TITLE, ORGANIZATION, ADDRESS, ZIP, PHONE

General Contractor

David R. Lane

David R. Lane & Associates

1312 Sixty-third Street,
Toledo, Ohio 43610
419/173-8777
Home: 419/176-0020

Electrical

Stanley T. Harris

Harris Electrical Co.

1121 Broadway
Central City, Ohio 43568
419/555-0321
Home: 419/040-5944

HVAC

Malcolm Squyres

Mechanical Systems Inc.

401 East Liberty
Lofton, Ohio 43454
419/042-0990
Home: 419/068-7767

Plumbing

John W. Ashby

Ashby & Sons

711 Sixty-third Street
Toledo, Ohio 43610
419/172-9335
Home: 419/555-4441

Figure 3-3 Project directory.

municating what needs to be done when. Before the intense activity on the project starts, the construction manager should draw flowcharts to identify who communicates with whom and graphically demonstrate how the various project procedures will work. The purpose is to record titles and identify key representatives of the owner, construction manager, architect, and contractors. A project directory, including home phone numbers for those problems that won't wait, should also be made (see Figure 3-3).

But a paper system can only go so far; a construction manager must talk to people. Face-to-face communication can expose many unidentified problems.

Organizing

The second step to successful project management deals with creating an organizational network and a set of procedures that unify the project team—so everyone is moving in the same direction, toward the same objectives.

1 *Initiate a project manual.* The construction manager and the key members of the project team (architect, engineer, owner, etc.) need project facts at their fingertips. A project manual puts them there. It is essentially a working file, containing both manual and automated reports to give a clear picture of the project's status.

A person's vital signs—blood pressure, temperature, pulse—measure health. The project manual's first function is to display the project's vital signs—quality, schedule, and cost. They must be as visible as the clipboard at the foot of a hospital bed. The project manual organizes the enormous amount of detail associated with construction projects; it acts as a checklist and reminds the project team that there is information to be obtained, recorded, and acted upon.

A side benefit: Most project arguments arise from misunderstandings. The likelihood of confusion is minimized when everyone has the same facts displayed in a project manual.

2 *Draw organization charts.* It's useless and exasperating to be the only ordered fragment in a sea of chaos. As the construction manager, you have to organize the entire project team, not just your own people. Assign clearly defined responsibilities to each member and establish a chain of command, integrating your people and procedures with those of the client (see Figure 3-4).

Because we're accustomed to the project-delivery process, construction managers forget how overwhelming construction can be to a newcomer. Again,

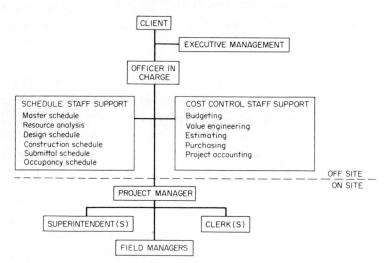

Figure 3-4 Project team.

when clients aren't experienced with construction programs and how they work, construction managers can help them prepare for the project not only by devising an organization chart for their staff, but by spelling out time demands, decisions that will have to be made, and information that must be gathered and circulated throughout the project. Confusion and delay will be avoided later if the client is "walked through" the steps to getting the project built and operating.

3   *Establish momentum.* New projects often take too long to get under way; you must catapult the project into action. If the pace is set at the beginning of the project, it's easier to maintain it. The "squatters" technique—intense brainstorming sessions between the client and project team, on site, at the beginning of a project—was initially developed by CRS to generate design programs, but it can be used to get construction off the ground, too.

4   *Prepare contractor manuals.* Contractors need a manual that tells them in their language, not a lawyer's, how the project is going to work. The contractor's manual contains some of the same information as the project manual, but the material is presented from the standpoint of how it will affect the contractor. It should outline the procedures for the control of submittals, transmittals, field orders, change orders, directives, approvals, on-site communication, inspections, and requests for payment. If you don't tell contractors specifically how a project is going to be run, they may assume that it will be run like their last project.

5   *Plan the work of inspection companies.* Qualified companies must be retained to provide soil and site

data, and to inspect and test concrete, welding, piping, soil compactions, etc. Decide with the client and the architect-engineer how they will be selected, what their responsibilities will be, and who will direct their work, pay them, and review their reports.

Monitoring

Construction management has come a long way. Computers have become integrally involved in the monitoring aspect of construction management services; things that were formerly determined by judgment and guesswork are now plotted and factored to minute detail with an amazing amount of precision. The construction management industry is justifiably proud of its management systems. But clients don't hire construction managers to marvel at intricate computer programs: they want a cost-effective project delivered on time.

In monitoring lies the real value of applying sophisticated data systems to the construction process. With accurate monitoring procedures, problems can be identified and corrected before they have a lasting effect on building progress. But just because a program schedules an activity doesn't mean it will get done. You have to pay attention to both the printouts and the real world and react immediately to any discrepancy between the two. Even the National Aeronautics and Space Administration (NASA), with all its computers, requires on-course corrections to hit the moon.

Project reporting should always be approached hierarchically, with the appropriate information (depending on how involved a person is in the project) routed to the appropriate team members. Different people associated with the project need different types and different amounts of information. A field manager will need to know when each change order was submitted and which contractor was delayed by rain on which day. An executive manager will need only summaries of, say, a month's activities and of any impending scheduling problems.

Some standard reports include:

- *Daily site reports*, which record weather, work done, personnel on site, and visitors. Their purpose is to settle arguments if a contractor doesn't provide enough workers or materials to keep the job on schedule or if claims arise (see Figure 3-5).

- *Weekly reports*, to summarize the week's activities and keep major issues visible (see Figure 3-6).

- *Monthly reports*, which summarize cost and schedule status and modification or completion of agreements. They usually contain a narrative that gives an overall comparison of the project's predicted and actual status and alert the management team to any potential problems (see Figure 3-7).

Every project is unique, so unique reports must be created to meet special needs. For example, for one overworked board chairman who was immensely interested in a project, we wrote a weekly one-paragraph "pulse report." It was a personal note from our project manager that kept the chairman up to date on the project and prevented the problems that an occasional visit from an uninformed but powerful client can cause.

SCHEDULE CONTROL

One of a construction manager's most important responsibilities is to finish a project on time. It's an old story: Time is money, and construction managers run a very

CM

DAILY REPORT   PROJECT

                                           DATE

To
From
Report Day
CC
Weather
Temperature   Hi   Low

VISITORS

WORK ACCOMPLISHED

Figure 3-5 Daily report.

```
┌─────────────────────────────────────────────────────────────────┐
│                            ⒸⓂ                                     │
│            ─────────────────────────────────────                 │
│    WEEKLY REPORT                   PROJECT                        │
│                                                                   │
│                                    DATE                           │
│            ─────────────────────────────────────                 │
│    To                                                             │
│  From                                                             │
│ Week Of                                                           │
│    CC                                                             │
│                                                                   │
│                                                                   │
│                                                                   │
│                                                                   │
│                                                                   │
│                                                                   │
│                                                                   │
│                                                                   │
│                                                                   │
└─────────────────────────────────────────────────────────────────┘
```

Figure 3-6 Weekly report.

CM

MONTHLY REPORT   PROJECT

DATE

From
Month Of
CC

OPERATIONS SUMMARY

COST SUMMARY

AGREEMENTS SUMMARY

COMMENTS

Figure 3-7   Monthly report.

tough race with inflation. You can better your chances of winning that race if you follow these steps:

1   *Conceive the strategy.* The first step in schedule control is building the project on paper. Again, this is best done after you have brainstormed approaches with the project team. The reason for collaboration? You want to enlist the prejudices, wisdom, and commitment of the owner, architect, and engineers. With these in mind, develop ten different delivery concepts and make ten variations on each.

It's dangerous to generalize, but we almost always phase design and construction. I've rarely seen a project that should be bid in one piece. Over and over again we've saved time and money and increased our control of the process with multiple contracts. The fundamental problems with fast-track are the risk and the anxiety created when construction is begun before all the bids have come in.

The solution is a prudent strategy that assures us all, step by step, of the proper results. A strategy addresses what the team feels are all the important issues and tasks. It shows their relationship to each other and their duration in proportion to the project's duration. A strategy is no guarantee, but a good strategy demonstrates that a project *can* be realized. It's a security check. A construction manager should always make sure the plan is there, that the project is controllable, and that the client is safe.

2   *Document the best strategy with a CPM schedule.* The critical-path method (CPM) of scheduling, shown in the network diagram of Figure 3-8, is a great test of logic. CPM systems provide discipline and handle the detail of complex strategies. But network

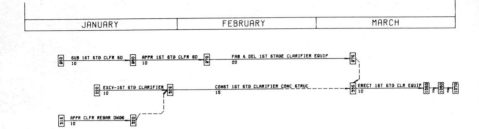

Figure 3-8 CPM schedule.

diagrams, on their own, are uninspiring; they can't be counted on to communicate. Summary bar charts are better for explaining strategies and for demonstrating to team members how their activities relate to real time (see Figure 3-9).

3 *Monitor, update, and enforce the schedule.* Even the best CPM schedule is useless unless it's administered

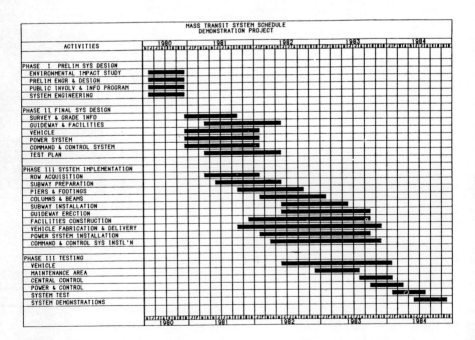

Figure 3-9 Summary bar chart.

with common sense and vigor, supplied by watchful, energetic managers. On construction projects out in the field, there is too much downtime between activities. One activity grinds to a halt, and the next is slow to get started. Without drive, delays develop. A construction manager must not only develop accurate schedules but must also keep on top of the schedules and make sure theory is transformed into reality.

You can't expect people to respond to computer reports. Computer printouts obscure problems in a fog of detail, and many people will resist the discipline and structure of a computer schedule. The big activities must be kept visible with summary charts, and the big issues must be handled with memos, letters, and person-to-person discourse. Without this kind of follow-through, a CPM diagram is likely to turn into a piece of wallpaper.

Many different types of schedules are involved in the project-delivery process. Here are some of them:

• *Master project schedule*. The master schedule is to construction management what schematic design is to architecture. It describes the total project-delivery concept. Developing that concept may be the most creative act in the construction management process.

The fuzzy and diverse ideas of the key team members are combined into one precise idea and translated into a CPM network diagram and then a summary bar chart schedule. The result is kept up to date throughout the project through periodic revisions (see Figure 3-10).

• *Design schedules*. CPM scheduling works as well for design as it does for construction. In fact, scheduling for design is probably more important than scheduling for

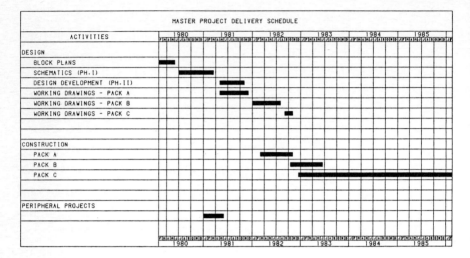

Figure 3-10   Master project-delivery schedule.

construction, since it's a lot easier to check progress on a construction site than in the A-E's office. The design schedule displays the decision sequence, labor requirements, the design-construction interface, and the lead time for client approvals.

The design schedule should be planned with the architect-engineer. As part of this stage, we figure labor hours for each activity and produce a graphic plot that sets up a manpower versus time available comparison. Then we play "what if" games with the computer until the schedule applies all the available resources effectively (see Figure 3-11).

• *Prebid schedules.* Plans and specs describe what is to be done; the prebid schedule describes when. A prebid schedule is mandatory for a multiple-contract project: including it in the plans and specifications means that contractors bid on cost, scope of work, and *time*. Prebid schedules inform the contractors how each one's job relates to the others', what their individual schedules

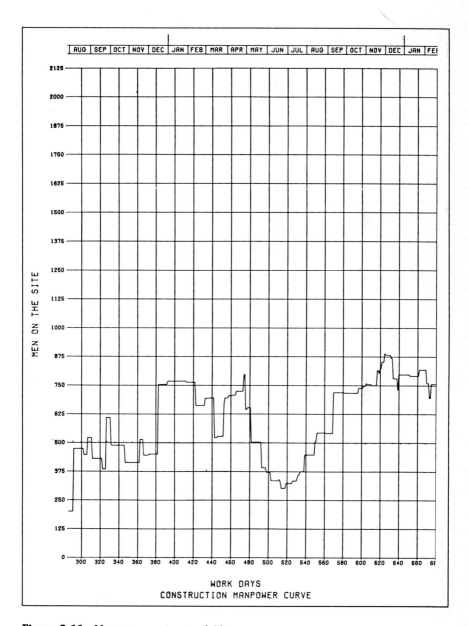

Figure 3-11   Manpower vs. time available.

are, and when they can expect delivery of prepurchased, long-lead-time materials. And they establish an enforceable schedule.

The only reliable way to make a liquidated-damages clause stick is with a detailed prebid schedule as part of the contract documents. Here's why: Most laws allow time extensions for delays caused by the owner or architect, acts of God, strikes, or other acts beyond a contractor's control. If the architect delays checking shop drawings, if the owner procrastinates on a change order, or if there is a trucking strike, the contractor can claim a time extension as compensation.

But a contractual prebid schedule often demonstrates that these occurrences don't in reality delay the critical activities. There's usually enough float time built into schedules to absorb a minor upset. The general conditions of every contractor's contract should state, *"Delays beyond the control of the contractor which can be absorbed by float time shall not be cause for time extension."*

In the private sector you almost always find contractors with pride in their reputation who will do their best to deliver; with these people you can forget the onerous liquidated-damages clauses. But in international and public work, where jobs are won on price alone and the bidders have lawyers review the specs for loopholes before bidding, it's wise to get all the protection available for the owner.

• *Submittal schedules.* Strange as it may seem, it's actually more important to schedule activities happening *off* the construction site. On-site construction activities are right there in front of you, but off-site activities are invisible and easily forgotten without scheduling systems. Many parts of a building are designed and constructed in a factory, packaged, shipped, and erected on site.

Once materials and labor are on site, construction is a fairly straightforward business. The tough part is getting it all together at the right time.

Before the project is under way, the construction manager can use the plans and specifications to make a list of everything that needs to be submitted for approval by contractors or manufacturers. The submittals should be scheduled and checked off as they're completed. Procurement schedules for long-lead items should include submittal dates and approval times, as well as dates for document production, requests for quotations, purchase orders, shop drawings, manufacturing, and shipping (see Figure 3-12).

A set of shop drawings or a material sample can go from manufacturer to subcontractor, to general contractor, to construction manager, to architect, and then around again. With so many handoffs, there are bound to be fumbles. Somebody has to keep an eye on the ball. That's you.

• *Construction schedules.* Don't expect contractors to want to work according to your prebid schedule. The prebid schedule is anonymous and preliminary; construction schedules are the refined versions of early concepts. As soon as the low bidder is known, expand the prebid schedule with that contractor's input. Contractors want to do things their own way; let them, if it's at all possible. A contractor's insight will make the schedule more accurate and probably cut the duration, and at the very least you'll enlist pride of authorship. Construction schedules should be updated regularly by using contractors' reports to reflect actual on-site progress. Too often they are not.

• *Short interval schedules.* Once the big picture is in view, you need detail to manage daily activity. Both the master schedule and construction schedules are general.

CM

SUBMITTALS REQUIRED

PROJECT   BUILDING A-3
ZONE 4

DATE   MARCH 1980

CONTRACT	REQ'D SUBMITTALS	DATE REQ'D TO CM	APPROVALS REQ'D	REQ'D RETURN DATE
C-2	Wood door shop drawings, samples	2 June 80	Arch.	16 June 80
C-2	Insulating security doors — mfr.'s product data, rough-in dwgs.	5 June 80	Arch.	19 June 80
D-1	Resilient flooring — 3 samples for each style	8 June 80	Arch.	22 June 80
D-4	Plumbing fixtures catalogue — 6 sets	16 June 80	Arch., mech. eng.	30 June 80
E-1	Switchgear manufacturer's technical data	18 June 80	Arch., elec. eng.	2 July 80

Figure 3-12 Submittals required.

100

Daily activities should be choreographed step by step through short interval schedules. Our version of the short interval schedule is a 2-week schedule drawn up by hand (see Figure 3-13). Each week it is "rolled over," dropping the completed week and projecting the next week's activities. Short interval schedules are proof that successful projects are done a day at a time, detail by detail.

• *Occupancy schedules.* It should be standard CM practice to take responsibility for getting clients settled into a new facility. Both the construction manager and the client frequently underestimate how difficult it is to get a project operational. In the past, some construction managers, including those at CM Inc., have made the mistake of assuming that their job is over when the last door is hung. But if things don't work, the users criticize the project and the client, who in turn can rightfully point to the people hired to manage construction on the project.

The people who use the building are important project participants. The occupancy schedule should be explained to them so they'll understand it and so you can take their needs and their anxieties into consideration. Construction doesn't usually shut down a client's operations, but moving into a new project can. When we finished one large hospital addition we had a crew of carpenters, plumbers, and electricians stand by during the move. We were transferring babies in incubators and intensive-care patients; all the new life-support systems had to work. Someone had to be there to do something about it if anything went wrong. Something usually does.

Expand the portion of the schedule dedicated to equipping, testing, occupying, and operating the building and

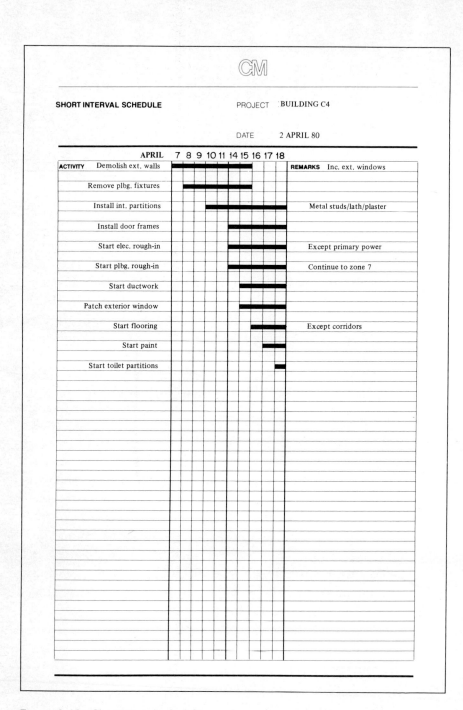

Figure 3-13 Short interval schedule.

then help the client manage it. Manufacturer's representatives should be on site for start-up, so they should be scheduled into occupancy activities. You can plot the movement of people and existing equipment to the new facility and schedule the first standard maintenance cycle. You can also set milestones for operations training and phasing out of the contractor's personnel.

COST CONTROL

Managing a client's money requires good judgment, advanced tools, and constant attention. It's a construction manager's most valuable contribution to a project. It's also the reason most clients hire construction managers. Construction management offers predictability, up-to-date market information, effective reporting systems, and a means of control, so cost control is much more than estimating. It has five equally important functions: budgeting, value engineering, estimating, procurement, and project accounting.

Budgeting

Budgets tend to be set too low. The client has a hard time facing what things really cost, like all of us when spending our own hard-earned money. And in selling the job, perhaps the construction manager hasn't really pressed the unpleasant facts about costs on the client. Nobody wants to be the villain in this act. But the way to be the hero at the end of a job is to be realistic about the budget from the start.

There are three critical rules for a budget: It's got to be right, what's in and what's out have to be defined, and categories must not change.

1   *Make it right*. Setting a budget too low is like skydiving without a parachute: everything is fine at the start of the trip, but it doesn't end well. On the other hand, an inflated budget creates the opposite problem: there's trouble before the project has a chance to take off. To make a budget accurate, you should depend on two processes.

The historical process draws on a file of past projects. It can be used in combination with a computer program that can take any category of these projects, allow for inflation, and factor the projects from where they were built to some other location. Automatically you know what an outpatient clinic built last year in Kansas City will cost at next year's prices in Anchorage or Albuquerque. *The analytical process*, on the other hand, enables you and the architect-engineer to hypothesize a building's geometry and systems, using standard space and equipment specifications. Then you can develop estimates as if design were complete.

Both processes are inexact. Ultimately comparisons and judgments have to be made. After that it's a matter of living with—and managing—the decisions.

2   *Define what is in and what is out*. Everyone involved in the project must know exactly what the budget covers, so it's essential to be specific and open about the items included from the start. What about fees? Interim financing? Owner's legal costs? Trouble is never far behind when you hear the words "Oh? I didn't know that was a part of the budget."

Our first project at CM Inc. was a high school. We actively marketed the bid packages and made sure there was competition for good prices. But after the first bids for early site work and structure came in, the superintendent was alarmed at how high they were. We thought they were right on target. It took quite a bit of discussion and backtracking to figure out the reason for the difference in our reactions.

We all knew what the total budget figure was, but we had different ideas about what it represented. The superintendent thought it would cover everything— construction; furnishings; testing; architect, engineer, and construction management fees; inspection; and legal fees. In this light, those first bids *would* seem way out of proportion. In our minds the same number covered construction only.

Besides knowing what's included, everybody must agree to and accept the budget down to the smallest item. A simple way to bring attention to the details is to ask the key team members to sign the final budget; although it may have no contractual meaning, people always read carefully documents that contain numbers before they sign.

3   *Establish permanent budgeting categories.* Our second project was a large hospital. Budget reviews were always chaotic, because budget categories changed between meetings. We could never refer back to the previous budgets. We not only lost control of cost problems, we couldn't even locate them.

The way to avoid this kind of confusion is to take time to plan the cost categories that can be reported on for the whole project, using past experience, foresight, and the contract structure that will eventually be used. Being consistent and hard-nosed about what goes where will keep budgeting problems identifiable and within a reasonable range. You must be able to refer to previous budgets—line by line—to control costs.

Value Engineering

Value engineering is a systematized, commonsense approach to saving money, a rigorous inspection of project systems and materials aimed at producing the greatest value for the least cost. But "value" has to be defined before it can be engineered. For every project, value can mean something different: it can mean front-end or life-cycle costs, prestige or function in a building, a tight schedule or a rock-bottom budget. Clients should rate the priorities for their own buildings: they must establish the values, and their construction managers might have to help them do it.

The best time for value engineering is *prior to design*. It is more efficient and less aggravating for the architect. Anyone can take potshots at final working drawings and specifications. It takes more knowledge and skill to help the A-E find potential savings and estimate a hypothetical design. This kind of collaboration minimizes conflict—and produces better buildings.

Value engineering should be a team effort to get an accurate prediction of cost-saving implications. It should involve the client, who understands the building's function; the architect-engineer, who understands the design alternatives; and the construction manager, who knows the cost of the design alternatives. To channel its efforts into areas with significant impact, the team needs a system to highlight the appropriate subjects for its scrutiny. Good budgeting formats establish *cost models*, or reasonable budget costs, for each building system. If a system as it's designed exceeds its cost-model budget, it's a good candidate for value engineering (see Figure 3-14).

Value engineering requires more than looking at isolated pieces of a project. Consequences have to be examined relentlessly—it's easy to save money on the structural system by making the beams deeper and lighter, but that makes the walls higher and therefore more expen-

CⱮ

COST MODEL COMPARISON

BREAKDOWN BY DISCIPLINE

PROJECT   GRANDEE CENTER

DATE   22 MAY 1980

ARCHITECTURAL	Model	Estimate	Variance	%
Exterior Wall	$1,500,000	$1,350,000		
Roof	800,000	310,000		
Floor	650,000	500,000		
Ceiling	2,300,000	2,420,000		
Interior Doors	350,000	332,000		
Interior Partitions	950,000	898,000		
Misc. Metals	20,000	18,000		
Painting	200,000	217,000		
Miscellaneous	70,000	70,000		
Total Architectural	$ 6,340,000	$ 6,115,000		
STRUCTURAL				
Excavation	$ 300,000	$ 318,000		
Reinforced Concrete				
Substructure	200,000	158,000		
Vertical Framing	925,000	903,000		
Horizontal Framing	1,300,000	1,273,000		
Miscellaneous	50,000	50,000		
Total Structural	$2,775,000	$2,702,000		
MECHANICAL				
Central Plant	$ 345,000	$ 324,000		
Packaged Units	200,000	215,000		
Piping & Accessories	192,000	205,000		
Air Distribution	452,000	440,000		
Complementary	17,000	18,000		
Miscellaneous	25,000	25,000		
Total Mechanical	$1,231,000	$1,227,000		
PLUMBING				
Equipment & Fixtures	$ 215,000	$ 225,000		
Piping & Accessories	175,000	152,000		
Fire Protection	76,000	88,000		
Complementary	23,000	28,000		
Miscellaneous	20,000	20,000		
Total Plumbing	$ 509,000	$ 513,000		
ELECTRICAL				
Primary Power	$ 75,000	$ 75,000		
Secondary Power	110,000	110,000		
Lighting	750,000	712,000		
Power Distribution	560,000	590,000		
Complementary	35,000	31,000		
Miscellaneous	50,000	50,000		
Total Electrical	$1,580,000	$1,568,000		

Figure 3-14   Cost-model comparison.

sive. The team has to determine what's most economical for the total project.

The second-best time for value engineering is after the bids come in: it's still early enough to incorporate savings without disrupting the schedule. A construction manager should make it a habit to ask the contractors who bid the job if they know of any ways to save money. Their experience, especially regional experience, will probably bring out a trick the design and CM team couldn't anticipate. Once an electrical bidder told us we could save $4000 if we changed a switch specification with a total cost of only $500. He explained that the local wholesaler wouldn't sell the switches without the wire and conduit, which he always overpriced. He was right.

Estimating

Estimates are produced throughout a project, but their purpose varies from one stage to another. At the start of a project, estimates help the client establish the budget; during design they put price tags on alternative building systems; before construction they predict the fair price for a bid; during construction they help price and negotiate change orders.

Computers help by organizing and processing detail, providing consistent formats, reducing feedback time from design to price, making it easy to update the budget, and reducing error. They can also perform other chores, like conversion of currency and measurement systems and computation of total labor-crew size. But not even a computer can predict low bids, no matter how accurate the cost data or how accurate the takeoff. And while estimates are essential information for predicting and tracking costs, *management* is what controls costs and what brings a project in on budget.

Estimating is scientific, figured with unit-cost files and inflation factors. Bidding is emotional. No computer can predict the emotions of bidders—whether one contractor or supplier is especially hungry, another anxious to build credibility in an area, one feeling too big to bother with a project, another concentrating on another size or type of job. "Estimate," as a noun, is defined as a judgment made by using mathematical calculations from incomplete data. Data on emotions are incomplete and always will be.

The precision of the estimating process far exceeds the accuracy of the assumptions. A computer carries out calculations to one one-thousandth of a cent, but contractors' markups for overhead and profit may vary by several percent of the project cost, depending on how much they want the job and how accurate their calculations are. Ditto for subcontractors and suppliers. Variations are compounded through several levels. And what's more, no two estimators will take off the same quantities, estimate the same equipment or labor, or assess the same risks.

So the best estimates are the result of good programs, good resources, experience, research, and some luck. No project-delivery strategy should depend on the estimates to be exactly right.

Procurement

Nothing ever has a fixed price. While shopping in one country where gold jewelry is sold by weight, I found that the price per ounce varied by as much as 20 percent from one shop to another. If the price of gold is an international standard and it has a 20 percent variation on one street on one day, think of the wiggle room in the price of construction, where so much depends on day-to-day

CHAPTER THREE 110

events. Moral: Be tough and analytical when you buy construction. There's always a price range. A construction manager's job is to find the rock-bottom price for the client.

Some cost-control feedback comes from estimating, but the best feedback comes from bids, so the earlier they come in, the better. It's not necessary to wait for all the drawings and specifications to be completed to start purchasing. If an item is over the budget, you can adjust and reduce costs through negotiating, changing the scope of work, or redesigning upcoming contracts.

Items should be checked off against the budget as they're purchased and the bottom line updated. If there is time and a fixed budget, the contracts don't have to be awarded until you've seen that the project can be completed within estimated costs.

No matter how tough the purchasing conditions, everyone loses if the construction manager accepts unfair prices. It obviously hurts the client. It's important too, for the bidders to know they can't get away with overpricing when you're on the job. If a client is inclined to accept out of expediency, you must explain that your reputation in the market is at stake.

Once we inadvertently let a specification go out that only one manufacturer could meet. The one and only bid came in 50 percent over our estimate. We changed the specification and bid it over two weeks later, making sure there was competition this time. When the bids came in we had one that was right on target, submitted by—guess who—the same manufacturer. Competition had cut his price by a third. You can't blame him for trying, but we would have been responsible if he had succeeded.

As a construction manager, you can save the client twice your fee through five good procurement procedures:

1 *Make a market analysis.* Know your territory. You can
go into a new community, spend two weeks gathering
facts, and know more about market conditions than
the local firms that have worked there for years and
assume they're up to date. I can say that from experience, because we've gotten overconfident, neglected
to do a market analysis, and been caught with outdated information in our own hometown.

Market analyses should be scheduled regularly, even
in a company's most active regions. A useful market
analysis will illustrate how to buy construction the
way local industry wants to sell it, how the work is
usually allocated and who does it most often, whether
the labor market is lean or fat, how local jurisdiction
will affect contract packages, when labor contracts
come due, and how great the bonding capacity of the
potential bidders is. Analyses will make sure the right
people are contacted and attracted to the job by showing you how to structure the work so it is inviting to
contractors. If paint and drywall are traditionally
combined in one contract in that region, it's going to
be cheaper and better to keep them together on this
job.

Market analyses need periodic updates, but a good
construction manager is constantly aware of who's out
there in the industry. The most satisfying way to save
money on construction is to find somebody who will
do the best job at the lowest price. Surprisingly, the
best work is often the cheapest, because constructors
who know what they're doing are both efficient and
accurate.

For international work, the world is the marketplace.
Getting the best price depends on knowing *where* to
buy. Up-to-date market research is essential because

the conditions change rapidly with world politics, currency fluctuations, and major shifts in supply-demand patterns.

2 *Buy strategically*. Bid packages are determined by answering three questions: What's urgent? What's easy? Where is compatibility needed?

Urgent materials get priority. If fabrication and delivery of steel is first on the CPM schedule, it should be bid first. Easy bids follow critical bids. Carpet may only be 1 percent of the total project cost; it's not urgent, but it can be easily bid with a one-page specification. And it means 1 percent more cost certainty.

Compatibility is also a reason for an early bid. For instance, most of a wastewater treatment plant is built around the process equipment. If that's not bid before the rest of the plant is designed, the engineer has two choices: to design around the equipment of one manufacturer and suffer the consequences of no competition, or to make the design so general, and therefore so expensive, that it will fit many brands. The obvious choice is to bid equipment first.

3 *Analyze vertical-horizontal purchasing trade-offs*. Many projects have more than one building. These jobs can be purchased either *vertically* or *horizontally*. In vertical purchasing, the work is divided into separate projects with a general contractor assigned to each. In horizontal purchasing, the project is divided into trade responsibilities: one contractor does all of the electrical work, another the plumbing, and so on (see Figure 3-15).

The benefit of vertical purchasing is that one person can be held directly responsible for the successful

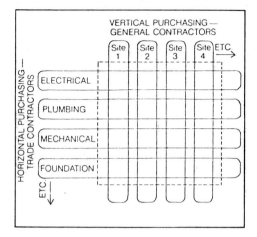

Figure 3-15 Vertical vs. horizontal purchasing.

completion of one piece of the project. Horizontal purchasing has two advantages: It reduces the total number of contractors on site and it gives each trade contractor increased purchasing power by way of volume discounts.

4 *Purchase long-lead items.* Often projects include material or equipment that causes months of delay before the contractor can start work. The potential delay items should be identified early and prepurchased. In developing countries the fact that most products must be imported creates more long-lead items. In fact, for some foreign projects *all* materials are long-lead. In some circumstances the best approach is to order all materials and equipment before awarding any construction contracts.

5 *Prequalify contractors if possible.* Contractors should be effectively evaluated with a rating system tailored to the needs of the project. The size of the project and the design will probably dictate most of the criteria used in the selection. If the design calls for a poured-

in-place skin and structural system there will be a high priority on contractors with a good reputation for concrete work. A "short list" of recommended bidders for each contract can save a lot of qualification time.

The selection of contractors for projects in developing countries should be based on their ability to perform in the international arena. Special skills might include purchasing, shipping, and expediting construction materials and equipment internationally; contracting for third-country labor; construction-mobilization facilities; housing, feeding, and caring for an entire labor and management force; providing bank guarantees; and dealing with different languages, customs, and religions.

Project Accounting

The fifth of the five cost-control functions deals with keeping tabs. In order to get where you're going, you have to know where you are and how you got there. Good project accounting gives the construction manager and the client an up-to-date, comprehensive view of the financial status and history of the project. It provides feedback for the people who must manage for results.

Our project-accounting system produces three basic reports that provide financial history, status, and progress for a project at both summary and detail levels: (1) the cost status report, which compares the latest estimate to complete the project with the budgeted amount; (2) the payment status report, which shows work completed by dollar value and by percentage of the total contract, and the balance on the contract; and (3) the contract detail status report, which shows the complete history of every line item in the accounting structure, including change orders approved and pending.

These are our standard reports, but almost every client wants to see the numbers presented differently. Project accounting systems, like all construction management tools, should be flexible enough to respond to each project's unique characteristics. As part of the early goal-setting and strategy-devising process, you should find out how clients want their financial track records set up. Then adjust the standard reports to reflect each client's particular concerns. Sometimes it will mean generating a completely new report; sometimes it will be simply a minor modification in format. This is one case where adaptability goes a long way. We've often learned from clients' reports that we thought were eccentric at first.

AGREEMENTS

A construction project generates a lot of agreements. Some are formal, written contracts; others are informal, but in effect just as binding. Enforcing agreements begins as a management process rather than a legal one; only when management fails does settlement end up in a court-room. The problem with all construction agreements, both oral and written, is that they are seldom drawn up by the people who do the work. Consequently contract conditions may not be communicated to the work force, and project teams may slip into contract violation out of ignorance. Communication problems like this can be avoided if the construction manager takes time to explain the contract's intent to the project team members and makes sure the agreements are updated and modifications are relayed to the site team.

If each person's duties are communicated to and understood by the whole team, then all team members know where their work begins and ends, how it is relevant to other operations, and what results are expected. The following policies will help to minimize problems with agreements.

1 *Record decisions on the spot.* Ever discuss a problem, reach a solution, and then discover that someone right beside you understood the decision differently? It's easily explained: No single thought is completely communicated and no one pays attention all the time. Also, people speak and listen from their own vantage point, toning and shading facts with their own interests.

   Putting all decisions in writing helps to clarify the confusion. Flowcharts and diagrams help illustrate thoughts and should be used to support oral and written communication. Record decisions as they're made and read them back to everybody on the spot. Don't go on until you see heads nodding.

2 *Review standard contracts carefully.* Standard agreements have been developed by the American Institute of Architects (AIA), the Association of General Contractors (AGC), the International Federation of Consulting Engineers (FIDIC), and other professional societies. They will always need modification for the next contract. They are often based on old contracts written for a linear construction process (where design, bidding, and construction administration are seen as finite and independent stages) and don't recognize the fact that these activities may be going on simultaneously. Also, contracts written by professional associations almost al-

ways favor their sponsors. A construction manager wants a contract that favors the client.

Every construction management firm should develop its own special clauses to address the issues of control and management and adapt standard contracts to the various project strategies. These clauses should supplement standard contracts on a project-by-project basis.

3 *Make an A-E–CM memo of understanding.* Normally there is no contract between the architect and the construction manager on a project. But because the two will be working together so much, it's important to spell out what each one plans to do for the other. It's also important to understand how the project responsibilities are divided and how they relate both timewise and taskwise. On one of our early projects at CM Inc., we worked for 9 months before we discovered that neither we nor the architect had contractual inspection responsibilities.

4 *Establish the need for insurance and legal counsel.* One part of the construction manager's job is to analyze and understand construction contracts, evaluate the risks involved on specific jobs, and make clients and contractors aware of all the provisions of a contract and its potential liabilities. But construction managers are not lawyers, CPAs, or insurance brokers. The other part of a construction manager's job is to make sure the client understands and gets the proper advice from these professionals.

Again, standard contracts must be examined in light of the legal and financial liabilities associated with multiple-contract construction. One of our early projects, a high school, was blown up by a tank car explosion. We had to build it again. Fortunately we got paid the second time around because we had advised the client to include construction management fees in his insurance coverage—not standard, because construction management wasn't standard.

5 *Monitor permit status.* Permits are agreements with a governing authority that allow you to do something if certain statutory conditions are met. Construction projects require all kinds of permits—for building, zoning, curbs, sewers, blasting, etc. They need to be researched and defined early in the project to prevent job delays. It's a construction manager's nightmare to be ready to start construction only to find that a blasting permit is needed and will take 2 months to process. On fast-track projects, arrangements frequently have to be made for special permit approvals. The reason? Most building permit authorities require complete working drawings for review, and that's not possible with fast-track projects, where site clearing and early construction often begin while the project is still in design.

The worst thing to do in these political situations is ignore the proper procedures or try to circumvent them. The best thing to do is get acquainted with the building code officials. Most of the time, if the fast-track concepts are explained to them, they can arrange to get the kind of documentation they need for approval. And these people aren't trying to obstruct progress or your success. Their responsibility is to protect the public interest. Be friendly.

6 *Make clear and specific contracts.* We've all heard people say they write contracts and then put them in a file drawer and forget them. They claim they operate on good faith. That's a noble idea but not very smart. Nobody likes people who quote contract technicalities, but the contract sets forth promises and it's essential to remember those promises—

whether they're made to you or by you. Review your own contract with the client at least once a month.

All agreements should spell out promises clearly with a minimum of legalese. A construction manager can help clients develop clarity in all project agreements. As I said before, standard forms are usually too general for the work at hand, so they must be adapted. But a word of caution about the old, wordy legal clauses that have stood the test of not only time but also the courtroom: Leave them alone. Just make sure everyone understands them.

7 *Document contract changes.* Projects take years to complete. Contracts are written by one generation of staff, implemented by a second, and finished by a third. The construction manager who best protects a client is the one who documents the contract changes meticulously.

But all the documentation in the world won't do a bit of good unless people are made aware of its implications. Again, it's the construction manager's responsibility to communicate changes and interpretations to the project team.

8 *Document how you have figured your fee.* Fee adjustments are often required during the course of a project. If the original fee calculation is available to the client, the logic for adjusting it is self-evident. Clients must realize that a construction manager's fee is set at a time when no one knows if the project will expand or contract. Careful, itemized documentation minimizes emotional negotiations that could damage rapport with the client just when teamwork is most important.

If a project is set up so that you are reimbursed for costs or services, establish a detailed budget and report against it on a monthly basis. If the estimate-to-complete changes, the client should be informed immediately—no surprises. It's good practice to calculate and tell the client early in the project what will be owed month by month, and to insist on prompt payments. It's good business. After all, a construction manager is hired to manage the client's money; you'll be respected for managing your own.

9 *Establish ground rules for change orders.* Project managers often issue directions that clarify or change the plans and specs or require resequencing of activities—under the assumption that there are no cost or schedule implications involved. A week later, surprise! The bill and a documentation of the delay or cost arrive from the contractor. With the right procedures, that won't happen. Make it clear from the start that there won't be change orders unless the terms are agreed on *before* work is begun. No retroactive changes. (Figure 3-16 shows a change-order proposal form.)

10 *Make change orders work for you.* The change order is the final documentation of an agreed-upon change (see Figure 3-17). It is the culmination of a request for quotation on a change and of a change-order proposal. Change orders, like the contract, the specifications, and the working drawings, are part of the overall contract between the owner and the contractor and should be treated as such. They require approval of the key project team members.

Contrary to popular opinion, change orders can be good, and a high number of change orders can be a sign of a well-run project. They are management tools. We have finished projects with more *deduct* change orders than *add* change orders. Deduct change orders result from opportunities to economize that come to light once construction is

CM

CHANGE ORDER PROPOSAL

PROJECT

DATE

From
To
Contract
Proposal #
CC

Please submit a proposal for the following changes in the contract

Estimate		Quantity & Units	Unit Cost	Total

Subtotal

Signed

Contractor

Date

% Overhead
% Insurance
% Tax
% Profit
Total Proposal Cost

This is not a change order or authorization to proceed with the proposed work

Figure 3-16 Change-order proposal.

CM

CHANGE ORDER

PROJECT

DATE

From
To
Contract
Change Order #
CC

The contract shall be changed as follows:

Reference
Documents

Payment for this change order shall fully compensate the contractor for all costs related in any way to this work and its effect on other work already contracted for,

Original Contract	$
Previous Change Orders	$
Current Contract	$
This Change Order	$
New Contract Total	$
Schedule Change	No. Days (+ −)

Authorized By	Accepted By
Signature	Signature
Organization	Organization
Date	Date

Figure 3-17 Change order.

under way. A contractor who has been asked to make money-saving suggestions probably will.

Most contractors dislike change orders and the paperwork they entail. But some contractors are delighted with change orders because they think they'll be able to charge more than is fair. These contractors are under the impression that when a change order comes up, they deserve a special bonus for the hassle. They don't—they deserve a fair profit. Whether a change order is a deduct or an add change order, ask the contractor to document the cost proposal in detail. Then negotiate the change with the detailed information at hand.

Let clients know they can expect both add and deduct change orders, and allocate a contingency fund. If you can effect changes that produce the same or better results for a client, and at the same time help a contractor, do so.

11 *Use directives sparingly.* Occasionally, it is necessary to give a contractor directions which increase the budget or extend the schedule, and because of the urgency of the work, there is not time to negotiate and process a detailed change order. When this occurs, a directive should be issued setting forth the change. The cost or time extensions can be negotiated later, but lids or maximums should be established if possible and the terms and method of calculating the change should be spelled out. The authority to issue directives should be discussed with the client early in a project, but there is always time for a phone conversation to confirm that the directive is agreeable before it is issued.

12 *Record every transmittal.* No conscientious executive would send a letter without filing a copy. Yet there is a lot of information that contractors, clients,

CM

CERTIFICATE	PROJECT BUILDING B-1
SUBSTANTIAL COMPLETION	ZONE 4
	DATE 3 JULY 1980

Contractor   Hiatus Corporation
Contract   B-11

The work performed under this contract has been reviewed and found to be substantially complete. The date of substantial completion is designated as 21 June 1980

The designated area or scope of work is   HVAC systems, Building B-1, Zone 4

This date does not represent the commencement of any warranties or guarantees under the conditions of the contract. All warranties and guarantees for all completed subsystems shall commence at final completion of the total building as specified by the Architect and Construction Manager.

The Date of Substantial Completion of the work is the date certified by the Architect and approved by the Construction Manager when construction is sufficiently complete in accordance with the contract documents, to allow for the uninterrupted start and completion of subsequent subsystems in accordance with the Construction Schedule.

A list of items to be completed or corrected, prepared by the Construction Manager and verified and amended by the Architect, is attached. The failure to include any items on such list does not alter the responsibility of the Contractor to complete all work in accordance with the Contract Documents.

REMARKS

2 working days ahead of schedule

REFERENCE DOCUMENTS

Original contract: B-11
Change orders: B-11-01, B-11-02, B-11-03

Signature	Signature	Signature
CM	Architect	Owner
CM Inc., Constructors/Managers		
Date	Date	Date
3 July 1980	3 July 1980	3 July 1980

Figure 3-18 Certificate of substantial completion.

and construction managers send around on a project that isn't typed on an 8½- by 11-inch sheet of paper—drawings, specs, material samples, computer printouts, diagrams, etc. A copy of a transmittal form serves as a record that these items were sent from one person to another.

13 *Formalize the sign-offs.* Contractors should be told when they're finished through a certificate of substantial completion, used with precision by the construction manager (see Figure 3-18). Too many jobs linger on for years, when a project should wind up with as much energy as it started with.

TEAMWORK

Companies don't do things, people do. And it's a lot easier to get things done with people you like. People want team members who can be counted on to be honest, do their bit, and enjoy it in the process. Don't let people on your team bad-mouth the client, the architect, and associates, or the contractors. It's usually defensive, always in bad taste, and even if it's true it only makes things worse. Good and bad, feelings are almost always reciprocated: the best way I know to find out how well a client likes our project manager is to find out how well the project manager likes our client.

Sometimes clients or contractors act unreasonably. But staying reasonable when others aren't is a part of a construction manager's job. Often clients are anxious about their projects: it's their money, and their jobs may be on the line. If this is a person's first construction project, the pressure will most likely produce some signs of strain.

And when things go wrong, insecurity causes people to place blame on others rather than focus on the solution. In order to get everybody out of this defensive frame of mind, it may be wise to accept a little more blame than you feel you deserve. As a construction manager, you need to convince the client and the team that you're confident and capable of getting the job done.

Contracts can't cover all eventualities. The world's biggest projects are the most uncertain. The focus of a construction manager's work is cost and schedule management; the architect's focus is design. Because construction management contracts don't call for design work, it's easy to assume that it's none of your business. The fact is construction managers should support *all* of the client's project objectives, not just those for which they have contractual responsibility.

The team members' contractual relationship is inconsequential to a genuine team concept. It doesn't matter whether an architect has a prime contract with the clients or is under subcontract to the construction manager. The architect should feel an obligation to serve the client, and you as construction manager should use your skills to encourage all involved to pool their resources. When you are subcontracted to the architect or engineer, make sure all of you realize you share the same goals— the client's.

Most important, a construction manager should make the client part of the team. Figure out what role the client wants to play: it can be quarterback, coach, or an involved spectator with a heavy bet on the outcome of the game.

It's also good policy to do more than the contract calls for on joint ventures. Human nature being what it is, if all partners do more than what they think their share is, it will come out about right. Some people will take advantage, but others will reciprocate. You will form long and profitable relationships with them.

4

CM
SUPPORT
SYSTEMS

Managing a successful construction project requires judgment, vigilance, and the ability to work with people. But computers play an important role in bringing order to the construction process. They provide checks for completeness and logic, integrate minute but essential detail, and improve communication among the team members by displaying the same information in a consistent format for everyone to absorb on a routine basis.

We developed our own data systems for control of our projects—and our specialty is construction, not computers. Thus they are tools created by their users, well suited to the realities of construction. And because we created them, it is easy for us to adapt them to the unique requirements of new clients and new projects. Understanding how the programs work and how they go together and maintaining flexibility in packaging them are the keys to a successful construction management computer-support system. We modify our programs and our services for almost every job.

Our first computer system was initiated in 1963 with what we believe was the first computer-based construction-cost estimating system in the industry. Today our cost-control systems routinely provide the project team with precise, consistently organized data for comparing building costs throughout design and construction. Our scheduling systems, based on the critical path method (CPM), enable us to create useful, accurate schedules quickly. The alphanumeric reports give precise, detailed information, while the graphic reports illustrate the information in a clean, simple format that's readily understood.

No doubt these systems make our lives easier and our work more exact and predictable. All of the records and all of the detail bring more precision to what used to be educated guesswork, which benefits both the client and us. The pitfall of computer systems is their tendency to obliterate the big issues with detail and develop groups of people who get more interested in the intellectual elegance of the system than in the practical results. It is an enthusiastic project team that makes the systems work. The input and the responses to the output are entirely dependent on their judgment and their ability to respond.

The discussion that follows revolves around our support systems, whose capabilities and structure are similar to many CM companies' programs today. They will illustrate some of the ways computers can work in the construction management process.

SCHEDULING

Throughout a project, thousands of activities occur simultaneously and sequentially, involving countless people and products from countless locations. The whole development of construction management has been in conjunction with finding ways to speed construction, which usually means more people working at once, which requires more sophisticated schedules. A physical picture that shows how the activities relate and what consequences they bring is the first and perhaps most essential step in planning project delivery. A "master schedule" can be developed for construction only, but it is most effective when it incorporates design activities as well as construction.

Most people in the construction industry, including us, prefer critical path method (CPM) scheduling. The printout from a CPM program is a list of all the project's necessary activities—and a computer-plotted, time-scaled network diagram that shows the relationships between them. With CPM reports, the construction manager—along with the owner, architect, contractors, subcontractors, manufacturers, and suppliers—has a clear view of where a project is, where it ought to be, and where everyone fits in.

Every project entails numerous types of schedules: the master schedule, reflecting overall strategy; and many design, procurement, and construction phase schedules in varying levels of detail. Each of these schedules may also be produced many times to reflect changing conditions, so there will probably be several revised versions of the same schedule. Keeping the latest schedules in front of all the right people is a task in itself.

Scheduling Input

A CPM system is a logical discipline used first to record and then to analyze schedules. For input it requires a list of activities needed to accomplish a project. ("Project" can be defined as an entire design and construction sequence; just design or just construction; or some part of either.) The activity list also sets forth the duration and sequence of the activities associated with the project. The system is dependent on people at this point to theoretically build the project on paper; this planning amounts to a walk-through of the schedule.

Any activity required for design or construction will demand resources such as money, quantities of building materials, or labor hours. On our system, as we list the activities required to execute a project, we can associate as many as five resources; and reports on each of the five resources can be generated, either as they're required, as they're consumed, or both.

The resources we associate with the activity reflect the client's concerns. Examples of resources we would track routinely might be money, labor hours, building materials, or equipment. But one owner might want to keep tabs on how much gasoline is consumed on a project; and on international projects, we usually estimate the need for labor housing.

Various codes can also be assigned to each activity. Possibilities include an organization code to clarify who is responsible for each activity (owner, architect, city, subcontractor, construction manager); location codes for either broad parameters (such as the city in which the activity will occur) or narrow parameters (such as the floor on which the activity will occur). Bid-package codes can be assigned to assist in devising a bidding or procurement strategy. And activities can be given a graphic organization code to help define their location in the system's graphic output, to simplify visual comprehension.

In summary, the program input is a list of activities required to do a job. Associated with each activity are the following issues:

- Duration: How long will it take?

- Sequence and relationship: What must be done first? What must be done at the same time?

- Resources: What (usually money, labor hours, materials) is required to do the job?

- Responsibility: Who will do it?

- Location: Where will it be done?

- Bid package: How will it be bought and paid for?

- Graphic location: Where is it located on a bar chart?

Scheduling Program

With this input, the scheduling system's program finds the *critical path*—the sequence of activities that, if started as soon as possible, will set the overall duration of the project. For those activities not part of the critical path, the program calculates how much delay is possible without affecting the project completion date.

In addition, these programs can select, sort, categorize, and structure the input data in literally an infinite variety of ways, depending on the needs of the project team. We can get a printout of all the activities that begin on the week of June 9 to 14, a list of the plumbing contractor's tasks, or a display of only the essential finish dates.

Scheduling Output

The scheduling program is capable of producing two kinds of reports, which differ in the way they display the information. Alphanumeric reports are detailed listings; they describe several dimensions of every activity. Graphic reports display the activities by name only, but their positions on the drawing graphically represent their relationship to the construction schedule and to each other in a way that is usually easier to comprehend than an alphanumeric report.

Three examples of the alphanumeric reports the system can produce are the schedule report, the scheduled cost report, and the resource-flow report.

Schedule reports (see Figure 4-1) help monitor progress on a project by listing for each activity its description; its *I* and *J* nodes (symbols of the beginning and end points of the activity within the logic of the equipment); the line number, which is where the activity appears on the plotted graphic reports; the work status, which indicates

```
CM CONSTRUCTORS/MANAGERS INC., SUITE 2200.
2700 S. POST OAK ROAD.  HOUSTON, TEXAS 77056.   (713) 622-5030
                                                                    DEMONSTRATION PROJECT
SCHEDULE CONTROL SYSTEM

SCHEDULE REPORT - TOTAL PROJECT EARLY START                     UPDATE #  12          DATA DATE:
NETWORK IC: PROMOA79              SEQUENCE: ERLYSTRT                    RUN # 90             REPORT DATE:
  I     J   LINE  WORK ACTIVITY DESCRIPTION              CONTRACT  ORG  REM  %      E A R L Y            L A T E          FLOAT
NODE  NODE  NO.                                          CODE      DUR  DUR  COMP   START    FINISH      START   FINISH
 5000  5005  142       AWD SITE PREP & EARTHWORK          OWNR     10    0  100%  21MAR79A  04APR79A  STARTED  FINISHED    0
 5030  5035  145       PROVIDE SAFETY EQUIPMENT           CM        5    0  100%  04APR79A  11APR79A  STARTED  FINISHED    0
 5010  5015  144       PROVIDE STAFF HOUSING              CM       10    0  100%  04APR79A  18APR79A  STARTED  FINISHED    0
 5020  5025  142       PREPARE CONSTRUCTION SCHEDULE      CM       10    0  100%  18APR79A  02MAY79A  STARTED  FINISHED    0
 5040  5045  144  STR  CLEARING SITE                      R1SITE    5    0  100%  02MAY79A  09MAY79A  STARTED  FINISHED    0
 5050  5055  142  CMP  CLEARING SITE                      R1SITE    5    0  100%  09MAY79A  16MAY79A  STARTED  FINISHED    0
 5060  5065  145  STR  EXCAVATION                         R1SITE   10    0  100%  09MAY79A  23MAY79A  STARTED  FINISHED    0
 5090  5095  144  STR  SITE GRADING                       R1SITE    5    0  100%  16MAY79A  23MAY79A  STARTED  FINISHED    0
 5100  5105  146  CMP  SITE GRADING                       R1SITE    5    0  100%  23MAY79A  31MAY79A  STARTED  FINISHED    0
 5070  5075  142  CNT  EXCAVATION                         R1SITE   10    0  100%  23MAY79A  07JUN79A  STARTED  FINISHED    0
 5140  5145  147       INSTALL SITE UTILITIES             C5PLMR   30    0  100%  23MAY79A  06JUL79A  STARTED  FINISHED    0
 5176  5177   0        ELECTRICAL UNDERGROUND             C6ELEC   27    0  100%  05JUN79A  13JUL79A  STARTED  FINISHED    0
 5110  5115  145  STR  LAYOUT BLDG                        R1SITE    5    0  100%  07JUN79A  14JUN79A  STARTED  FINISHED    0
 5060  5085  144  CMP  EXCAVATION                         R1SITE   10    0  100%  07JUN79A  21JUN79A  STARTED  FINISHED    0
 5178  5179   0        MECHANICAL UNDERGROUND             C4MECH   22    0  100%  12JUN79A  13JUL79A  STARTED  FINISHED    0
 5120  5125  145  STR  SUBSTRUCTURE EXCAVATION            R1SITE    5    0  100%  21JUN79A  28JUN79A  STARTED  FINISHED    0
 5086  5088  142       INSTALL STORM/SANI DRAINAGE        C5PLMR   15    0  100%  21JUN79A  13JUL79A  STARTED  FINISHED    0
 5130  5135  144  CNT  SUBSTRUCTURE EXCAVATION            R1SITE    5    0  100%  28JUN79A  06JUL79A  STARTED  FINISHED    0
 5150  5155  149  STR  FOUNDATIONS                        R2CONC    7    0  100%  28JUN79A  10JUL79A  STARTED  FINISHED    0
 5170  5175  146       INSTALL UNDERGROUND UTILITIES      C5PLMR   10    0  100%  28JUN79A  13JUL79A  STARTED  FINISHED    0
 5146  5148  144       BACKFILL                           R1SITE    5    0  100%  13JUL79A  20JUL79A  STARTED  FINISHED    0
 5160  5165  149  CMP  FOUNDATIONS                        R2CONC   10    0  100%  13JUL79A  27JUL79A  STARTED  FINISHED    0
 5180  5185  150  STR  FORMING SLAB                       R2CONC   10    0  100%  27JUL79A  10AUG79A  STARTED  FINISHED    0
 5200  5205  151  STR  POURING SLAB                       R2CONC    7    0  100%  10AUG79A  21AUG79A  STARTED  FINISHED    0
 5190  5195  149  CMP  FORMING SLAB                       R2CONC    7    0  100%  10AUG79A  24AUG79A  STARTED  FINISHED    0
 5220  5225  150  STR  COLUMNS                            R2CONC    7    0  100%  21AUG79A  30AUG79A  STARTED  FINISHED    0
 5210  5215  151  CMP  POURING SLAB                       R2CONC    7    0  100%  21AUG79A  05SEP79A  STARTED  FINISHED    0
 5240  5245  152  STR  FORM SLAB AND BEAM 1ST FLR         R2CONC   10    0  100%  30AUG79A  14SEP79A  STARTED  FINISHED    0
 5236  5238  149       FORM AND POUR SHEARWALLS    FLR1   R2CONC   15    0  100%  30AUG79A  21SEP79A  STARTED  FINISHED    0
 5230  5235  153  CMP  COLUMNS                            R2CONC    7    0  100%  05SEP79A  14SEP79A  STARTED  FINISHED    0
 5260  5265  150  STR  POUR SLAB 1ST FLOOR                R2CONC    7    0  100%  14SEP79A  25SEP79A  STARTED  FINISHED    0
 5250  5255  151  CMP  FORM SLAB AND BEAM 1ST FLR         R2CONC   10    8   20%  21SEP79A  05NOV79   STARTED  05NOV79     0
 5280  5285  149  STR  COLUMNS 2ND FLOOR                  R2CONC    7    0  100%  25SEP79A  04OCT79A  STARTED  FINISHED    0
 5290  5295  152  CMP  COLUMNS 2ND FLOOR                  R2CONC    7    0  100%  04OCT79A  15OCT79A  STARTED  FINISHED    0
 5270  5275  149  CMP  POUR SLAB 1ST FLOOR                R2CONC    7    0  100%  05OCT79A  16OCT79A  STARTED  FINISHED    0
 5276  5278  150       FORM AND POUR SHEARWALLS    FLR2   R2CONC   15    1   93%  05OCT79A  25OCT79   STARTED  09NOV79    11
 5300  5305  151  STR  FORM SLAB AND BEAM 2ND FLOOR       R2CONC   10    4   60%  16OCT79A  09NOV79   STARTED  09NOV79     0
 5320  5325  150  STR  POUR SLAB                          R2CONC    7    7    %   09NOV79   27NOV79   09NOV79  27NOV79     3
 5310  5315  149  CMP  FORM SLAB AND BEAM 2ND FLOOR       R2CONC   10   10    %   09NOV79   27NOV79   09NOV79  27NOV79     0
 5330  5335  150  CMP  POUR SLAB                          R2CONC    7    7    %   27NOV79   06DEC79   27NOV79  06DEC79     0
 5340  5345  151  STR  COLUMNS 3RD FLOOR                  R2CONC    7    7    %   27NOV79   06DEC79   27NOV79  06DEC79     0
 5350  5355  149  CMP  COLUMNS 3RD FLOOR                  R2CONC    7    7    %   06DEC79   17DEC79   06DEC79  17DEC79     0
 5360  5365  155  STR  FORM BEAM AND ROOF                 R2CONC   10   10    %   06DEC79   20DEC79   23JUN40  08JUL80   138
```

Figure 4-1   Schedule report.

```
CM CONSTRUCTORS/MANAGERS INC., SUITE 2200,
2700 S. POST OAK ROAD, HOUSTON, TEXAS 77056,  (713) 622-5030
                                                              DEMONSTRATION PROJECT
SCHEDULE CONTROL SYSTEM

SCHEDULE REPORT - CONCRETE CONTRACT EARLY START                 UPDATE # 12        DATA DATE:
NETWORK ID: PROMOA79                SEQUENCE: ERLYSTRT           RUN # 90           REPORT DATE:
  I    J   LINE  WORK ACTIVITY DESCRIPTION           CONTRACT  ORG  REM    %      E A R L Y        L A T E          FLOAT
 NODE NODE  NO.                                        CODE    DUR  DUR  COMP   START   FINISH   START   FINISH

5150 5155 149 STR FOUNDATIONS                        B2CONC     7   0  100%  28JUN79A 10JUL79A STARTED FINISHED    0
5160 5165 149 CMP FOUNDATIONS                        B2CONC    10   0  100%  13JUL79A 27JUL79A STARTED FINISHED    0
5180 5185 150 STR FORMING SLAB                       B2CONC    10   0  100%  27JUL79A 10AUG79A STARTED FINISHED    0
5200 5205 151 STR POURING SLAB                       B2CONC     7   0  100%  10AUG79A 21AUG79A STARTED FINISHED    0
5190 5195 149 CMP FORMING SLAB                       B2CONC    10   0  100%  10AUG79A 24AUG79A STARTED FINISHED    0
5220 5225 150 STR COLUMNS                            B2CONC     7   0  100%  21AUG79A 30AUG79A STARTED FINISHED    0
5210 5215 151 CMP POURING SLAB                       B2CONC     7   0  100%  24AUG79A 05SEP79A STARTED FINISHED    0
5240 5245 152 STR FORM SLAB AND BEAM 1ST FLR         B2CONC    10   0  100%  30AUG79A 14SEP79A STARTED FINISHED    0
5236 5238 149     FORM AND POUR SHEARWALLS    FLR1   B2CONC    15   0  100%  30AUG79A 21SEP79A STARTED FINISHED    0
5230 5235 153 CMP COLUMNS                            B2CONC     7   0  100%  05SEP79A 14SEP79A STARTED FINISHED    0
5260 5265 150 STR POUR SLAB 1ST FLOOR                B2CONC     7   0  100%  14SEP79A 25SEP79A STARTED FINISHED    0
5250 5255 151 CMP FORM SLAB AND BEAM 1ST FLR         B2CONC    10   8   20%  21SEP79A 05NOV79  STARTED 05NOV79     0
5280 5285 149 STR FORM SLAB AND BEAM 1ST FLR         B2CONC     7   0  100%  25SEP79A 04OCT79A STARTED FINISHED    0
5290 5295 152 CMP COLUMNS 2ND FLOOR                  B2CONC     7   0  100%  04OCT79A 16OCT79A STARTED FINISHED    0
5270 5275 149 CMP POUR SLAB 1ST FLOOR                B2CONC     7   0  100%  05OCT79A 16OCT79A STARTED FINISHED    0
5276 5278 150     FORM AND POUR SHEARWALLS    FLR2   B2CONC    15   1   93%  05OCT79A 25OCT79  STARTED 09NOV79    11
5300 5305 151 STR FORM SLAB AND BEAM 2ND FLOOR       B2CONC    10   4   60%  16OCT79A 09NOV79  STARTED 09NOV79     0
5320 5325 150 STR POUR SLAB                          B2CONC     7   7    %   09NOV79  20NOV79  14NOV79 27NOV79     3
5310 5315 149 CMP FORM SLAB AND BEAM 2ND FLOOR       B2CONC    10  10    %   09NOV79  27NOV79  09NOV79 27NOV79     0
5330 5335 150 CMP POUR SLAB                          B2CONC     7   7    %   27NOV79  06DEC79  27NOV79 06DEC79     0
5340 5345 151 STR COLUMNS 3RD FLOOR                  B2CONC     7   7    %   27NOV79  06DEC79  27NOV79 06DEC79     0
5350 5355 149 CMP COLUMNS 3RD FLOOR                  B2CONC     7   7    %   06DEC79  17DEC79  06DEC79 17DEC79     0
5360 5365 155 STR FORM BEAM AND ROOF                 B2CONC    10  10    %   06DEC79  20DEC79  23JUN80 08JUL80   130
5357 5359 152     FORM AND POUR SHEARWALLS    FLR3   B2CONC    15  15    %   06DEC79  31DEC79  18JUN80 10JUL80   135
5520 5525 162 STR EXTERIOR WALLS (PRECAST PANELS)    H2CONC    25  25    %   17DEC79  24JAN80  26MAR80 30APR80    69
5380 5385 153 STR POUR ROOF                          B2CONC     7   7    %   20DEC79  03JAN80  08JUL80 17JUL80   138
5370 5375 155 CMP FORM BEAM AND ROOF                 B2CONC    10  10    %   24JAN80  24JAN80  10JUL80 24JUL80   128
5390 5395 156 CMP POUR ROOF                          B2CONC     7   7    %   24JAN80  04FEB80  24JUL80 04AUG80   128
5530 5535 160 CNT EXTERIOR WALLS (PRECAST PANELS)    B2CONC    25  25    %   24JAN80  28FEB80  30APR80 05JUN80    69
5540 5545 161 CMP EXTERIOR WALLS (PRECAST PANELS)    B2CONC    25  25    %   28FEB80  03APR80  05JUN80 11JUL80    69
6066 6068 178     FINISH CONC FLOOR                  B2CONC    10  10    %   27MAR80  10APR80  03APR80 17APR80     5
```

Figure 4-2 Schedule report: concrete contract.

whether the activity is started, current, or completed; the contract code; the originally scheduled duration of the activity; its remaining duration; the percentage of the activity that is complete; early and late start and finish dates; and total float time, which is how long the activity can slip without affecting the project completion date. An optional report shows free float time, which tells how much time can elapse without affecting any other activities.

The schedule report can show all of the project's activities, as Figure 4-1 does, or a restricted list selected by a specific code such as site location or a certain contractor. This enables a manager to easily pinpoint the progress of work in very narrow terms. Figure 4-2 is a listing confined to the activities of the concrete contractor. It can be seen from this schedule that there are 11 days of float time for forming and pouring shear walls for floor 2—11 days of wiggle room before the rest of the schedule is held up by the delay. One thing, though, to keep in mind with these kinds of printouts is the context: The first activity of the concrete contract occurs only *after* the preparatory activities have been completed by the owner, the construction manager, and the site and plumbing contractors.

Scheduled-cost reports are tools for monitoring resource allocation. The report shown in Figure 4-3 gives the schedule and cost information on each activity by listing the activity's *I* and *J* nodes, work status, description, contract code, scheduled start and finish dates, remaining duration, contract cost, percentage complete (which can be updated independently of schedule information), and cost expended to date or this month. The report can be sorted by any data field required—by contract or by work area, for example. It will produce subtotals at selected breaks followed by a summary.

CM CCNSTRLCTORS/MANAGERS INC., SUITE 2200,
2700 S. PCST OAK ROAD, HOUSTON, TEXAS 77056, (713) 622-5030

SCHEDULE CONTROL SYSTEM — DEMONSTRATION PROJECT

SCHEDULED COST REPORT - CONTRACT COST BREAKDOWN — UPDATE # 12 — DATA DATE: 24OCT79

NETWORK ID: PROMOA79 — SEQUENCE: I-JLOGIC — RUN # 90 — REPORT DATE: 30OCT79

I NODE	J NODE	WORK ACTIVITY DESCRIPTION	CONTRACT CODE	SCHEDULED DATES START	SCHEDULED DATES FINISH	RMN DUR	CONTRACT COST	PCT COMP	COST TO DATE	COST THIS MONTH
5040	5045	STR CLEARING SITE	B1SITE	02MAY79A	09MAY79A	0	10,976.00	100%	10,976.00	
5050	5055	CMP CLEARING SITE	B1SITE	09MAY79A	16MAY79A	0	10,976.00	100%	10,976.00	
5060	5065	STR EXCAVATION	B1SITE	09MAY79A	23MAY79A	0	42,826.95	100%	42,826.95	
5070	5075	CNT EXCAVATION	B1SITE	23MAY79A	07JUN79A	0	42,826.95	100%	42,826.95	
5080	5085	CMP EXCAVATION	B1SITE	07JUN79A	21JUN79A	0	42,826.95	100%	42,826.95	
5090	5095	STR SITE GRADING	B1SITE	16MAY79A	23MAY79A	0	8,024.10	100%	8,024.10	
5100	5105	CMP SITE GRADING	B1SITE	23MAY79A	31MAY79A	0	8,024.10	100%	8,024.10	
5110	5115	STR LAYOUT BLDG	B1SITE	07JUN79A	14JUN79A	0	2,001.67	100%	2,001.67	
5120	5125	STR SUBSTRUCTURE EXCAVATION	B1SITE	21JUN79A	28JUN79A	0	41,061.82	100%	41,061.82	
5130	5135	CNT SUBSTRUCTURE EXCAVATION	B1SITE	28JUN79A	06JUL79A	0	41,061.82	100%	41,061.82	
5146	5148	BACKFILL	B1SITE	13JUL79A	20JUL79A	0	33,521.33	100%	33,521.33	
		Summary →	TOTAL	02MAY79A	20JUL79A	0	284,127.69	100%	284,127.69	
5150	5155	STR FOUNDATIONS	B2CONC	28JUN79A	10JUL79A	0	143,779.00	100%	143,779.00	
5160	5165	CMP FOUNDATIONS	B2CONC	13JUL79A	27JUL79A	0	143,779.00	100%	143,779.00	
5180	5185	STR FORMING SLAB	B2CONC	27JUL79A	10AUG79A	0	35,222.33	100%	35,222.33	
5190	5195	CMP FORMING SLAB	B2CONC	10AUG79A	24AUG79A	0	35,222.33	100%	35,222.33	
5200	5205	STR POURING SLAB	B2CONC	10AUG79A	21AUG79A	0	43,996.00	100%	43,996.00	
5210	5215	CMP POURING SLAB	B2CONC	24AUG79A	05SEP79A	0	43,996.00	100%	43,996.00	
5220	5225	STR COLUMNS	B2CONC	21AUG79A	30AUG79A	0	97,513.00	100%	97,513.00	
5230	5235	CMP COLUMNS	B2CONC	05SEP79A	14SEP79A	0	97,513.00	100%	97,513.00	
5236	5238	FORM AND POUR SHEARWALLS FLR1	B2CONC	30AUG79A	21SEP79A	0	386,428.00	100%	386,428.00	
5240	5245	STR FORM SLAB AND BEAM 1ST FLR	B2CONC	30AUG79A	14SEP79A	0	289,337.00	100%	289,337.00	
5250	5255	CMP FORM SLAB AND BEAM 1ST FLR	B2CONC	21SEP79A	05NOV79	8	289,337.00	20%	57,867.40	
5260	5265	STR POUR SLAB 1ST FLOOR	B2CONC	14SEP79A	25SEP79A	0	377,623.33	100%	377,623.33	
5270	5275	CMP POUR SLAB 1ST FLOOR	B2CONC	05OCT79A	16OCT79A	0	377,623.33	100%	377,623.33	377,623.33
5276	5278	FORM AND POUR SHEARWALLS FLR2	B2CONC	05OCT79A	25OCT79	1	386,428.00	93%	359,378.04	359,378.04
5280	5285	STR COLUMNS 2ND FLOOR	B2CONC	25SEP79A	04OCT79A	0	97,513.00	100%	97,513.00	97,513.00
5290	5295	CMP COLUMNS 2ND FLOOR	B2CONC	04OCT79A	15OCT79A	0	97,513.00	100%	97,513.00	97,513.00
5300	5305	STR FORM SLAB AND BEAM 2ND FLOOR	B2CONC	16OCT79A	09NOV79	4	291,052.57	60%	174,631.54	174,631.54
5310	5315	CMP FORM SLAB AND BEAM 2ND FLOOR	B2CONC	09NOV79	27NOV79	10	289,337.00	0%		
5320	5325	STR POUR SLAB	B2CONC	09NOV79	20NOV79	7	377,623.33	0%		
5330	5335	CMP POUR SLAB	B2CONC	27NOV79	06DEC79	7	377,623.33	0%		
5340	5345	STR COLUMNS 3RD FLOOR	B2CONC	27NOV79	06DEC79	7	97,513.00	0%		
5350	5355	CMP COLUMNS 3RD FLOOR	B2CONC	06DEC79	17DEC79	7	97,513.00	0%		
5357	5359	FORM AND POUR SHEARWALLS FLR3	B2CONC	06DEC79	31DEC79	15	386,428.00	0%		
5360	5365	STR FORM BEAM AND ROOF	B2CONC	06DEC79	20DEC79	10	289,337.00	0%		
5370	5375	CMP FORM BEAM AND ROOF	B2CONC	10JAN80	24JAN80	10	289,337.00	0%		
5380	5385	STR POUR ROOF	B2CONC	20DEC79	03JAN80	7	377,623.33	0%		

Figure 4-3 Scheduled cost report.

Figure 4-3 tracks cash allocation and is sorted by contract. Read from top to bottom, it tells us that the site preparation (contract B-1) for the project is complete and the concrete work (contract B-2) is under way; it also tells us that the forming and pouring of shear walls on floor 2 is 93 percent complete and will be finished in one day's time. We can also see the cost status compared with the contracted costs. The summary tells us that the site contract (B-1) was scheduled to run from May 2 to July 20, that it is totally complete, and that its cost of $284,127.69 was right on target and paid in full at least as early as the previous month.

A construction manager would review this schedule with the various trade contractors individually, making reasonableness checks on the allotted times and contract cost.

Another example of the scheduling program's alphanumeric reports is the resource-flow report, which relates resource consumption to time. By linking the cost-control system, the procurement system projection, and the scheduling system, it creates a demand projection and control tool for the project's total resources. The report can project the demand for workers, cash flow, equipment, and materials, for instance, on a daily or monthly basis.

Figure 4-4 shows the cash flow for the entire project and for the concrete contract. The concrete monthly cash flow projects a heavy cash demand from September 1979 through January 1980, dropping sharply the following month—an indication that the bulk of the concrete work will be done during that 5-month period. The total project monthly cash flow example shows that in December 1979, at the same time most of the concrete work is complete, there will be another surge in cash flow. This is when the trade contractors will begin work on the contract.

```
 DEMONSTRATION PROJECT
                                        DISTRIBUTION BY TIME            NETWORK ID: PROMOA79
                                        TOTAL PROJECT MONTHLY CASH FLOW    DATE: 30OCT79   69

 ---------------------------------------------------------------------  UPDATE# 012 19OCT79  247
         I                 MONTHLY                    I
 MON   I----------------------------------------------I--------------------------------------
         I                                            I                CUMULATIVE
 ---------------------------------------------------------------------
 MAY79      133093                                    I        133093
 JUN79      440139                                    I        573233
 JUL79      711217                                    I       1284450
 AUG79     1127046                                    I       2411497
 SEP79     1118612                                    I       3530110
 OCT79     1583697                                    I       5113808
 NOV79     1112755                                    I       6226563
 DEC79     3686436                                    I       9913000
 JAN80     4630670                                    I      14543470
 FEB80     4884016                                    I      19427687
 MAR80     2584922                                    I      22012609
 APR80     1956864                                    I      23969473
 MAY80      884246                                    I      24853720
 JUN80      433029                                    I      25286750
 JUL80      117460                                    I      25404210
 AUG80       65961                                    I      25470172
 SEP80       55030                                    I      25525202
```

(a)

```
 DEMONSTRATION PROJECT
                                        DISTRIBUTION BY TIME            NETWORK ID: PROMOA79
                                        B2 CONC - CONCRETE MONTHLY CASH FLOW  DATE: 30OCT79   69

 ---------------------------------------------------------------------  UPDATE# 012 19OCT79  247
         I                 MONTHLY                    I
 MON   I----------------------------------------------I--------------------------------------
         I                                            I                CUMULATIVE
 ---------------------------------------------------------------------
 JUN79      41079                                     I        41079
 JUL79     257044                                     I       298124
 AUG79     348488                                     I       646613
 SEP79    1118612                                     I      1765226
 OCT79    1294360                                     I      3059587
 NOV79    1112755                                     I      4172342
 DEC79    1515266                                     I      5687609
 JAN80    1191737                                     I      6879347
 FEB80     554870                                     I      7434217
 MAR80     568024                                     I      8002241
 APR80     204274                                     I      8206515
```

(b)

Figure 4-4 Resource-flow report for (a) total project and (b) concrete contract.

Construction managers and the client use these three alphanumeric reports (the schedule report, the scheduled cost report, and the resource-flow report) to budget the various resources. Financing and labor needs are determined by these types of schedules. Sometimes, too, they point out a problem; for instance, on a remote site, there might be a demand for more laborers at one point than there are accommodations for. The options are to change the schedule or to arrange for more housing during this period.

Graphic reports are simply visual displays of the information contained in the alphanumeric reports. They lay out complicated activity sequences step by step, and they also give overviews of the project's progress. Each of the three graphic programs we use satisfies a different project or scheduling need. For example:

• *Network diagrams* (Figure 4-5) give the schedulers prompt verification of the information they have fed into the computer, which would be difficult to obtain from a printed report. The diagrams also serve as presentation-quality communication tools which we can have in our hands within hours of the schedule's finalization.

The network diagrams are produced by giving the system a schedule model from a similar project and code

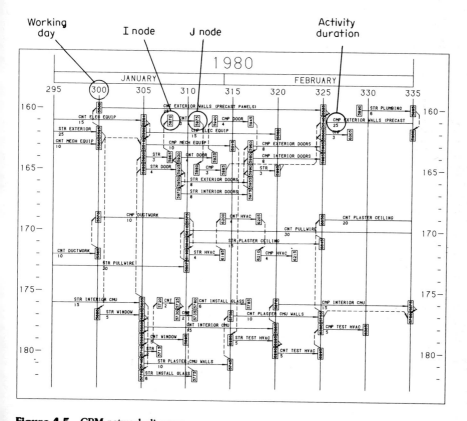

Figure 4-5 CPM network diagram.

information to guide their organization. The rest is automated. The system then generates instructions, which are stored on a tape; the tape drives the plotter, which in turn produces the drawing of the time-scaled network.

In Figure 4-5 the intersection of lines 169 and 315 shows a point where the installation of the heating, ventilation, and air-conditioning (HVAC) systems will be under way (current). Tracing line 315 (which represents the three hundred fifteenth working day on the project) vertically will reveal what else will be going on simultaneously. On this project, that includes work on the interior and exterior doors, the plaster ceiling, glass installation, and initial tests on the HVAC system.

• *Summary bar charts* (as in Figure 4-6) provide a summary of the schedule in a graphic, easily understood format. They are quickly produced from network diagrams. But even though bar charts are far more easily understood than network diagrams, they are usually

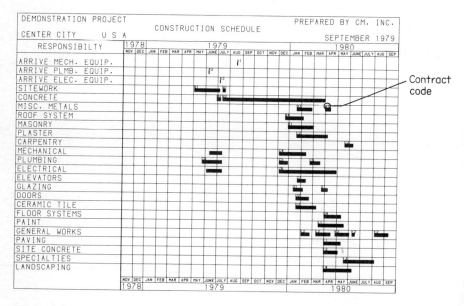

Figure 4-6 Summary bar chart.

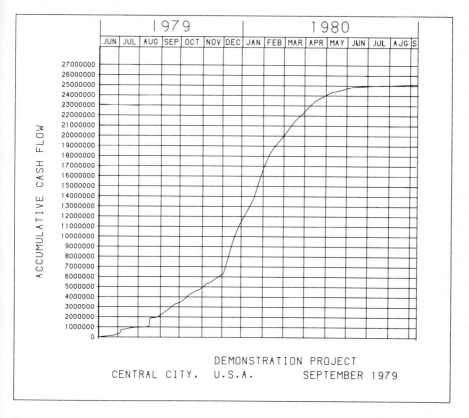

Figure 4-7 Resource-flow plot.

poor tools for scheduling day-by-day construction, because they can't incorporate all of the details. They are actually simplistic representations of a very complicated process. But this is also where their usefulness lies—in the overview they give of the schedule.

• *Resource-flow plots* (see Figure 4-7) show the impact time and resource considerations have on one another. They show peaks and valleys of resource needs, such as labor requirements; and using the picture they draw, we can adjust the activities that use those resources to produce a less erratic, more even demand flow. This increases efficiency and minimizes transitional strain.

We can develop resource plots on an incremental or a cumulative basis for any of the resources we initially associated with each activity. For instance, if we decided we wanted to track the mechanical contractor's labor requirements, we could ask for a plot on the total duration of the particular contract, or only for the month of May. The curve in Figure 4-7 is for cash flow over a 15-month period. You can see that there will be a few cash demands made sporadically through August, that they will become more regular and intensify through May, and that by June they will level off at $25 million. This means that all the equipment and labor will be on site by then; this is what we call the *peak activity period*. When demobilizing starts, the cash flow curve will drop, again sporadically at first, tapering off to the final punch-out stages.

BUDGETING

There are two methods we use to establish a reasonable budget for a project: historical and analytical (see Figure 4-8). The cost results of our experience—estimating, purchasing, bidding, and managing billions of dollars worth of construction—are stored in an automated data file, and this serves as the basis of our historical method. A computer program named BLITZ retrieves these data and applies them to the parameters of new and potential projects.

The BLITZ data file is arranged according to building type. Each listing contains a code name and number for each project; whether the data came from our estimate or from bids; the midconstruction date; the project's area in square feet; and the percentage of that square foot cost represented by architectural, structural, mechanical,

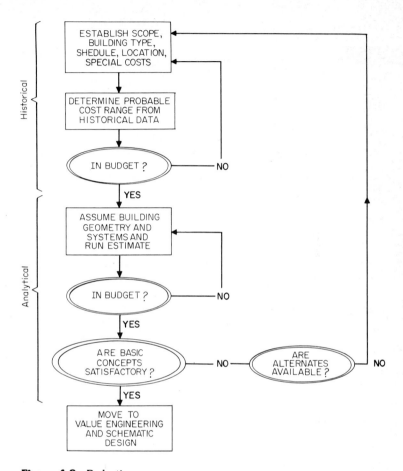

Figure 4-8 Budgeting process.

plumbing, electrical, conveying, and service equipment. Fixed equipment, site preparation, and special foundations are listed as a percentage of the total square foot cost.

Using each project's actual midconstruction date, the program escalates the project's cost to any future date requested by the project team. The program also averages the projects on a square footage basis—figuring, for instance, rates for projects larger and smaller than 100,000 square feet, as in Figure 4-9. The bottom section

```
CM CONSTRUCTORS/MANAGERS, INC.    2700 SOUTH POST OAK ROAD, SUITE 2200    HOUSTON, TEXAS 77056    (713) 622-5030
COST CONTROL SYSTEM
HISTORICAL COST REPORT                                                                                  7 NOV 79

COMPLETE LISTING - USA NATIONAL AVERAGES        PERCENTAGES AND COSTS BASED ON BIDS AND ESTIMATES             PAGE: 1

MEDICAL FACILITIES     - HOSPITAL          - CONSTRUCTION MANAGEMENT
     COSTS ADJUSTED TO MID-CONSTRUCTION  0/19 0 WITH A LOCATION FACTOR OF 1.000
                                            *--------- % OF BUILDING COST ---------*  BLDG COST/ *-- % ADD-ONS --*    COST/      SF/
                                    AREA    ARCH  STRC  MECH  PLBG  ELEC  CONV  SERV      SF    FXEQ  SITE  SFDT        BED       RFD
     ACUMA  3102  EST   6/1976    55300.SF  32.8  17.5  18.2  14.0  17.5   0.8   0.0   378.85  13.7  13.8   0.0    523757.   1382.50
     ARKHO  3102  BID   6/1974    77472.SF  30.3  18.3  20.6  13.7  13.9   3.2   0.0   291.79   9.0   1.8   0.0    213261.    730.87
     BAHAI  3102  EST   7/1973    56943.SF  29.6  18.5  19.5  12.5  14.1   5.8   0.0   263.85   0.0   7.0   0.0    166936.    632.70
     BLOHO  3102  BID   2/1975   190552.SF  34.5  19.5  16.0  10.2  14.4   5.4   0.0   268.13  18.2   9.0   0.0    241002.    898.83
     CAPHO  3102  BID  11/1976    95445.SF  31.7  21.1  20.6  10.6  13.8   2.2   0.0   399.40   7.9   6.7   0.0    544581.   1363.50
     FRANK  3102  BID   2/1978   188246.SF  22.1  23.7  24.3   9.0  20.7   1.2   0.0   295.62   8.2   9.2   0.4    309158.   1045.41
     GUAHM  3102  BID   5/1975   145345.SF  26.7  28.5  14.5  12.9  15.1   2.8   0.0   328.52  16.0  10.8   0.0    318327.    968.97
     HAIDA  3102  EST   7/1973    81081.SF  37.6  13.6  17.2  12.2  16.9   7.5   0.0   264.70  18.1  14.2   0.0    178853.    675.67
     HAIHT  3102  BID   6/1973    65085.SF  43.1  12.9  17.9  10.8  13.0   7.3   0.0   270.26  14.4  14.4   0.0    159906.    591.68
     HERMM  3102  BID   4/1974   466053.SF  37.3  21.2  13.7   8.7  15.7   3.4   0.0   317.37   7.7   1.6   0.6    528263.   1664.47
     HOPEA  3102  BID   9/1974    37020.SF  24.8  38.9  14.2  11.2  10.0   0.9   0.0   351.34   6.4   4.0   0.0    433552.   1234.00
     LAWTN  3102  BID   2/1974    97400.SF  35.7  24.0  13.3   9.2  14.0   3.8   0.0   301.00  13.4   6.9   0.0    458081.   1521.87
     MARYS  3102  BID   1/1978   208493.SF  30.5  21.7  18.6  11.1  16.2   1.9   0.0   313.35   6.3   3.1   0.0    257213.    820.84
     NAPPI  3102  EST   6/1976    77800.SF  37.0  19.1  16.5  12.9  14.5   0.0   0.0   324.50  18.2  10.4   0.0    450824.   1389.29
     ROCHO  3102  BID   3/1976   204658.SF  26.5  29.1  20.4   7.4  13.0   3.6   0.0   345.42   9.2   8.5   0.0         0.      0.0
     SALBY  3102  BID   1/1977   269823.SF  25.9  22.7  20.1   9.4  17.6   4.3   0.0   269.05  11.1   4.6   1.0    212267.    788.06
     SOUTH  3102  BID   8/1975   286971.SF  23.5  23.8  17.9  10.1  18.8   5.9   0.0   356.59   6.3   3.9   0.0    465144.   1304.41
     TUXON  3102  BID   4/1974    51250.SF  25.1  22.4  21.8  11.6  17.2   1.9   0.0   413.18   5.9   6.6   0.0         0.      0.0

  LESS THAN 100000.SF  10 JOB AVG  69480.SF  32.8  20.6  18.0  11.9  14.5   2.8   0.0   375.89  11.9   8.6   0.0    347750.   1058.01
  100000.SF OR OVER     8 JOB AVG 245018.SF  28.3  23.7  18.2   9.8  16.4   3.6   0.0   311.76  10.4   6.3   0.7    333053.   1070.33

           COMPLETE    18 JOB AVG 147497.SF  30.8  22.0  18.1  11.0  15.3   3.2   0.0   319.61  11.2   7.6   0.7    341320.   1063.60

  LOW RANGE (-10%)      5 JOB AVG 132697.SF  34.1  17.4  18.1  11.0  15.2   4.1   0.0   267.20  15.4   9.8   1.0    191793.    717.57
  MID RANGE            9 JOB AVG 166943.SF  30.0  24.9  17.3  10.7  14.7   2.6   0.0   318.77  10.5   6.3   0.5    371084.   1177.01
  HIGH RANGE (+10%)     4 JOB AVG 122242.SF  28.3  21.2  19.6  11.6  16.8   3.3   0.0   387.00   8.4   7.7   0.0    511160.   1350.14
```

Individual projects

Range, ft², avg. / avg.

Figure 4-9 Sample BLITZ report.

represents average costs for all projects as divided into low-, middle-, and high-range costs.

BLITZ is designed to provide a reasonable cost range for a new project based on experience and factored to when and where the project will be built. But detailed questions about each specific project must be addressed to make a budget accurate. Is it to be built out of granite or stucco? Is it a simple rectangle in the middle of an open field, or is it a complex building added to an existing building, distorted into a difficult geometry by a tight site in a congested central business district?

After the building systems, materials, and geometry have been discussed, and before design begins, an analytical method can be used to hypothesize the design and produce an estimate from often broad parametric cost data. These data are compared with the data resulting from the historical BLITZ program, and after applying some final judgment, the budget is set.

VALUE ENGINEERING

Value engineering is not a science but a process. Its purpose is to get the most project for the money in the project budget—not only in terms of initial cost but also in terms of life-cycle cost (initial + operating + periodic replacement cost).

Too often value engineering is used just for reducing the costs of a project that has already run over budget. Usually in these cases the targets for value engineering are items like finishes, cladding, landscaping, and other things that might be called frills. They are easy to cut out or scale down, with a consequent reduction in cost (and often quality). But that's not the real purpose of value engineering. Value engineering is supposed to make a design more effective by locating waste and substituting cost-effective options. Eliminating landscaping and all other parafunctional costs is not the purpose or the sense of value engineering.

To be most effective, value engineering should be scheduled before design (see Figure 4-10). Construction managers and contractors should help architects choose the right systems and materials and build value *into* the project. This is another instance where field experience and knowledge of the latest developments in the market are invaluable, and often much backtracking and evaluation time can be avoided by identifying cost-saving items on the front end.

The way to approach value engineering is by exception. It is impractical to examine every detail of a project. You need a system to comb out major items that are exceeding reasonable limits so you can devote your attention to them. The reference point for what defines "reasonable" is most likely the historical version of the cost data file.

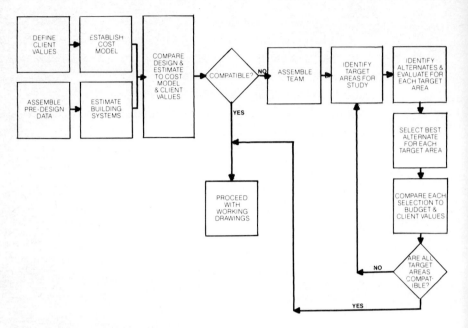

Figure 4-10   Value engineering process.

Although hundreds, perhaps thousands, of issues can be addressed in value engineering, energy consumption is by far the most important. During the life of most buildings the total energy cost will exceed the construction costs many times over. For most projects, utility costs will exceed mortgage payments within 10 years of their construction. Therefore the most important value engineering issue is how the building systems respond to energy operating costs.

Energy Value Engineering

We have computer programs which evaluate the effectiveness of energy conservation alternatives. They range from simple statistical reference data sources to comprehensive simulators (see Figure 4-11).

1 *EBUDG*. Architect-engineer design teams frequently spend much time and energy looking at conservation possibilities and alternative energy sources that are actually inappropriate for the project at hand. EBUDG provides direction to the design process by establishing a reasonable *energy budget* for the building (just as BLITZ provides a reasonable construction cost budget). It identifies major energy end uses. It is a historical data base with information on the types and rates of energy consumption in various climates and locations.

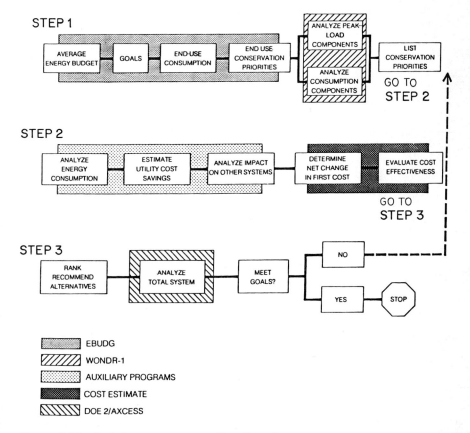

Figure 4-11 Analyzing energy conservation alternatives.

After we outline the building type and climatic zones, EBUDG breaks down the types of energy use to show us which areas the design team should concentrate effort on to realize the most effect. For example, some buildings in Houston use 50 percent of their energy demand on air conditioning, and so cooling techniques are a logical target for the design team.

The input for EBUDG consists of general climatic zone, area by usage type (for example, 10,000 square feet of office space, 50,000 square feet of warehouse), and the number of occupants anticipated. The output consists of two bar charts. One shows the 20th percentile, mean, and 80th percentile range of an energy budget for a typical building, modeled from our input. The scale is in Btu per square foot per year (see Figure 4-12).

The other chart shows a typical breakdown of energy usage by type. It illustrates what percentage of the total energy consumption will go for the various end uses such as lighting, cooling, and equipment operation (see Figure 4-13).

2 *WONDR-1*. It is difficult to determine the relative importance of internal loads (such as people and equipment) compared with the external loads placed on a building by the environment, solar radiation, and temperature. Designed to be run in series with

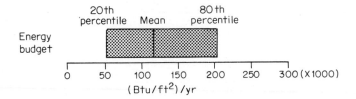

Figure 4-12 EBUDG output: energy-budget percentile scale.

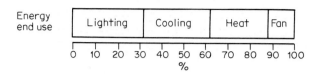

Figure 4-13 EBUDG output: energy consumption breakdown.

EBUDG, WONDR-1 analyzes how various components in a building contribute to overall energy consumption. WONDR-1 also introduces the concept of
time into the evaluation. By simulating a simple
hour-by-hour energy balance (or mix) for the building, the program shows how various load components
compare in time and average energy use.

If through EBUDG we determine that cooling is a
prime end use, WONDR-1 will show us how much of
the cooling load comes from the glass, the walls, the
ceilings, infiltration, etc. And we'll see how the peak-
load air conditioning relates volumewise and timewise to other end uses, such as lighting (see Figure
4-14). The program identifies those areas which will
benefit most from design engineering—so WONDR-1
amounts to another system for combing out the items
with real money-saving potential. Designers can use

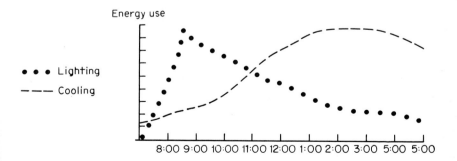

Figure 4-14 WONDR-1 output: energy mix by time of day.

WONDR-1 many times during conceptual design to understand the building's performance as a dynamic system.

For input, WONDR-1 needs hourly weather data—for a typical day, typical season, or typical year—and the best description of the building available. If the building's geometry and orientation are known, they can be used for input; if not, the program has default values for typical buildings.

The program's output comes in the form of either rainbow plots or pie charts, showing the time relationship between internal and external loads. WONDR-1 provides considerable information on how the building performs. Through running WONDR-1 a number of times, for example, we might see that an inch of sill height on the window will save as much energy as a meter of overhang on the building. The graphics also illustrate how effective economy controls would be in compensating for any broad-range variations in load. Through successive runs of WONDR-1, the design team often begins to develop an intuitive feel for the interaction of the various building systems.

3 *Auxiliary programs.* Because the input for WONDR-1 consists of hourly data, the precision of the program can be increased simply by using auxiliary programs to generate more and better hourly readouts for the different components of the building. Key design alternatives can also be evaluated through the supplementary programs. And the additional programs can be used with typical solar and weather data for typical *years,* to provide estimates of long-term average energy conservation potential.

We have seven auxiliary programs. Each addresses a different energy conservation problem.

COMPGLZ, a program designed to deal with glazing alternatives. Glazing questions are extremely complex, affecting many energy variables—solar gain, heating and cooling load, natural lighting. Also, there is a basic economic issue involved in the life-cycle value of double-glazed windows.

LUMEN II, a program directed at lighting. Lighting typically turns out to be the most important energy use in commercial buildings, so particular emphasis must be placed on high-efficiency systems that maximize the use of natural lighting.

EFFUFAC tackles the issue of energy-efficient walls. Opaque walls are often designed without regard to their orientation or function. There are many walls that actually use more energy when insulation is added to them. In a sunny, cold climate, for instance, a south-facing wall acts as a solar collector; insulation only detracts from the wall's collecting efficiency and increases the heating load. Also, in manufacturing plants and other buildings with very high internal loads, some of the process heat must be vented. Insulation may make this operation more difficult.

ECONZER evaluates the long-term effectiveness of various economy-control cycles and heat-recovery schemes.

SOLPAS, *SOLPUMP*, and *SOLWAT* combine to estimate the real cost-effectiveness of active and passive solar applications.

AXCESS predicts actual performance of HVAC systems in a given building—difficult even with a complete set of specifications.

DOE 2 assesses the energy effectiveness of the energy system and its design as a whole. Many state and federal agencies are requiring a total-system analysis such as this to determine if the building complies with energy conservation standards.

If the results of this energy value engineering process meet with the preestablished project energy goals, our energy design work is complete. If not, we back up, add to our list of alternatives, and run through the same evaluation procedure, until we arrive at one system that satisfies the client, the building goals, and the parameters of energy-conscious design.

ESTIMATING

Once design is under way, we produce definitive estimates in three categories: (1) by building system; (2) by contract; and (3) by the divisions set up for the Construction Specifications Institute (CSI). We do this (1) so the architect can select the most effective and economical building system, (2) so we can anticipate the contract prices, and (3) so the architect-engineer's specifications can be relayed to the trade contractors in terms accepted in the industry.

Detailed cost predictions are based first on quantities of specific building materials. These estimates are refined through the schematic-design, design-development, and contract-document stages to reflect new and updated information from the building team.

Estimating Input

Four types of input are used in our estimating system: unit-cost files, factors, quantity takeoffs, and resource files (see Figure 4-15).

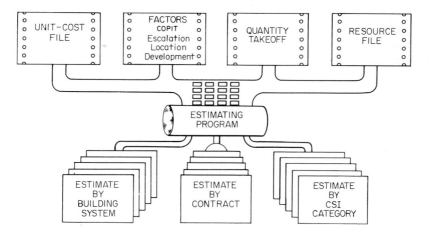

Figure 4-15 Estimating system.

We have both international and domestic unit-cost files, each with room for 35,000 unit costs of building components and materials and their descriptions and units of measure. The files are constantly updated. Each file uses a representative location within a specific country or region as a base for the unit costs.

With this system it's relatively easy to produce a unit-cost file for a new location. We assemble information on import duties, basic labor rates, and the price of locally produced staple materials. Those data plus standard information on the international price of materials and shipping costs give us a new unit-cost file for that location. We can go into any new region or country and know the costs of construction within days.

Our unit-cost files are more than simple price lists: they contain detailed and complete information on how the installed cost of a piece of equipment or material is determined. For example, if we wanted to know the price range for the various sizes of copper piping in a particular market, that information would be in the unit-cost file broken down into the material cost, labor cost, and

Material code

```
CM INC., CONSTRUCTORS/MANAGERS                              PLUMBING                                      30 OCT 79
1979                                                                                                      PAGE:    9
••••••••••••••••••••••••••••••••••••••••••••••••••••••••••••••••••••••••••••••••••••••••••••••••••••••••••••••••••
    CM                                                     MATERIAL        LABOR  SUBCONTRCT/      TOTAL CONTRACT     LAST
   ITEM  DESCRIPTION                          UNIT          COST            COST   EQUIP COST   UNIT COST ELEMENT   UPDATE
••••••••••••••••••••••••••••••••••••••••••••••••••••••••••••••••••••••••••••••••••••••••••••••••••••••••••••••••••••

PIPING AND ACCESSORIES
------------------------------------------------
   7631  PIPING-COPPER TYPE K W/FTGS & HGRS  1/2"  LF         1.010         2.170                     3.180    15065   MAY79
   7632  PIPING-COPPER TYPE K W/FTGS & HGRS  3/4"  LF         1.600         2.560                     4.160    15065   MAY79
   7633  PIPING-COPPER TYPE K W/FTGS & HGRS    1"  LF         1.940         3.040        .147         5.127    15065   MAY79
   7634  PIPING-COPPER TYPE K W/FTGS & HGRS 11/4"  LF         2.430         3.610        .147         6.187    15065   MAY79
   7635  PIPING-COPPER TYPE K W/FTGS & HGRS 11/2"  LF         3.050         3.870        .147         7.067    15065   MAY79
   7636  PIPING-COPPER TYPE K W/FTGS & HGRS    2"  LF         4.620         4.060        .147         8.827    15065   MAY79
   7637  PIPING-COPPER TYPE K W/FTGS & HGRS 21/2"  LF         6.760         4.470        .210        11.440    15065   MAY79
   7638  PIPING-COPPER TYPE K W/FTGS & HGRS    3"  LF         9.140         4.980        .262        14.382    15065   MAY79
   7639  PIPING-COPPER TYPE K W/FTGS & HGRS    4"  LF        15.400         5.920        .420        21.740    15065   MAY79
   7640  PIPING-COPPER TYPE K W/FTGS & HGRS        LS          .480          .490        .030         1.000    15065   MAY79
   7641  PIPING-COPPER TYPE K  (SOFT)               LS          .490          .490        .020         1.000    15065   MAY79
   7642
   7643  PIPING-COPPER TYPE L W/FTGS & HGRS  1/2"  LF          .890         2.060                     2.950    15065   MAY79
   7644  PIPING-COPPER TYPE L W/FTGS & HGRS  3/4"  LF         1.240         2.290                     3.530    15065   MAY79
   7645  PIPING-COPPER TYPE L W/FTGS & HGRS    1"  LF         1.710         3.000        .147         4.857    15065   MAY79
   7646  PIPING-COPPER TYPE L W/FTGS & HGRS 11/4"  LF         2.130         3.330        .147         5.607    15065   MAY79
   7647  PIPING-COPPER TYPE L W/FTGS & HGRS 11/2"  LF         2.870         3.830        .147         6.847    15065   MAY79
   7648  PIPING-COPPER TYPE L W/FTGS & HGRS    2"  LF         4.280         4.000        .147         8.427    15065   MAY79
   7649  PIPING-COPPER TYPE L W/FTGS & HGRS 21/2"  LF         6.320         4.330        .210        10.860    15065   MAY79
   7650  PIPING-COPPER TYPE L W/FTGS & HGRS    3"  LF         8.460         4.780        .262        13.502    15065   MAY79
   7651  PIPING-COPPER TYPE L W/FTGS & HGRS    4"  LF        14.200         5.660        .420        20.280    15065   MAY79
   7652  PIPING-COPPER TYPE L W/FTGS & HGRS        LS          .500          .480        .020         1.000    15065   MAY79
   7653
   7654
   7655
   7656  PIPING-COPPER TYPE M W/FTGS & HGRS  1/2"  LF          .720         1.930                     2.650    15065   MAY79
   7657  PIPING-COPPER TYPE M W/FTGS & HGRS  3/4"  LF         1.070         2.250                     3.320    15065   MAY79
   7658  PIPING-COPPER TYPE M W/FTGS & HGRS    1"  LF         1.360         2.780        .147         4.287    15065   MAY79
   7659  PIPING-COPPER TYPE M W/FTGS & HGRS 11/4"  LF         1.820         3.150        .147         5.117    15065   MAY79
   7660  PIPING-COPPER TYPE M W/FTGS & HGRS 11/2"  LF         2.460         3.760        .147         6.367    15065   MAY79
   7661  PIPING-COPPER TYPE M W/FTGS & HGRS    2"  LF         3.950         3.880        .147         7.977    15065   MAY79
   7662  PIPING-COPPER TYPE M W/FTGS & HGRS 21/2"  LF         5.420         4.090        .210         9.720    15065   MAY79
   7663  PIPING-COPPER TYPE M W/FTGS & HGRS    3"  LF         7.070         4.570        .262        11.902    15065   MAY79
   7664  PIPING-COPPER TYPE M W/FTGS & HGRS    4"  LF        12.720         5.540        .420        18.680    15065   MAY79
   7665  PIPING-COPPER TYPE M W/FTGS & HGRS        LS          .450          .530        .020         1.000    15065   MAY79
   7666
   7667  FOR EXTRA COPPER FITTINGS            ADD   LS          .200          .750        .050         1.000    15065   JUN77
   7668
   7669  PIPING - GALV STEEL W/FTGS & HGRS  1/2"  LF          1.050         1.920                     2.970    15065   MAY79
   7670  PIPING - GALV STEEL W/FTGS & HGRS  3/4"  LF          1.240         1.980                     3.220    15065   MAY79
   7671  PIPING - GALV STEEL W/FTGS & HGRS    1"  LF          1.430         2.076        .147         3.653    15065   MAY79
   7672  PIPING - GALV STEFL W/FTGS & HGRS 11/4"  LF          1.850         2.204        .147         4.201    15065   MAY79
   7673  PIPING - GALV STEEL W/FTGS & HGRS 11/2"  LF          2.190         2.547        .147         4.884    15065   MAY79
   7674  PIPING - GALV STEEL W/FTGS & HGRS    2"  LF          2.950         3.160        .147         6.257    15065   MAY79
   7675  PIPING - GALV STEEL W/FTGS & HGRS 21/2"  LF          4.340         3.950        .210         8.500    15065   MAY79
   7676  PIPING - GALV STEEL W/FTGS & HGRS    3"  LF          5.160         4.580        .262        10.002    15065   MAY79
   7677  PIPING - GALV STEEL W/FTG & HGRS     4"  LF          7.910         5.620        .420        13.950    15065   JUN79
```

Figure 4-16   Unit-cost file.

equipment cost for installation, with a total unit cost calculated for the product in place.

The costs listed in Figure 4-16 for 2-inch type L copper piping are general, or average, costs. To make the prices more specific to a particular project, we would have to research and apply the cost effects of local conditions. So, besides using the unit-cost file as input, an estimator depends on *factors* to relate the raw costs to a particular project. As illustrated in Figure 4-17, these include:

1   *COPIT*, a factor for figuring a contractor's overhead, profit, insurance, and taxes. It is based on our analysis of current market conditions affecting the project.

2 *Area location factor*, derived from published indexes, research on local market conditions, and our experience. It reflects local labor costs, productivity, and material prices. By applying the area location factor to our national average unit costs, we can figure a unit cost for any place in the United States. Area location factors for our overseas markets enable us to figure unit costs for international locales in the same manner.

3 *Development factors.* These are provisions for project growth during design and working drawings. Most clients, architects, and engineers think of things to add to the project (and thus increase the price of the project) as it progresses through design. The development factor is a sort of "hunch factor" that allows our estimators to make assumptions based on their experience. Our hunch factors depend on the architect and the client.

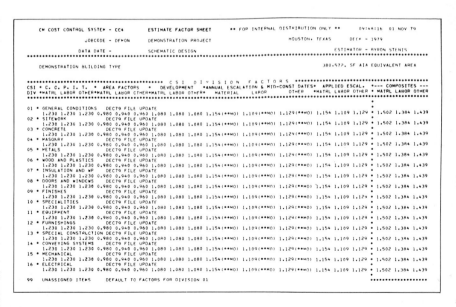

Figure 4-17 Factor sheet.

4 *Escalation*, a factor for anticipated inflation. Normally it is figured to the midconstruction date for each category of work.

On the basis of these factors, our system comes up with a composite number which, when used in conjunction with our unit-cost file, will reflect accurate prices for an individual project in a particular location at a particular time.

The next form of input for the estimating program is the *quantity takeoff* (see Figure 4-18). When we begin a project, the materials and quantities required for construction are determined from design drawings, from discussions with the architect and engineer, and from our estimators' experience in dealing with incomplete drawings. Material prices are retrieved from the unit-cost file by means of the material code number, and the quan-

CM INC., CONSTRUCTORS/MANAGERS   2700 SOUTH POST OAK ROAD, SUITE 2200   HOUSTON, TEXAS 77056   (713) 622-5030   01 NOV 79
COST CONTROL SYSTEM   ESTIMATOR: BYRON STENIS   CM FORMAT   PAGE: 11

DEMONSTRATION PROJECT   HOUSTON, TEXAS
SCHEMATIC DESIGN

THIS ESTIMATE WILL INDICATE VARIOUS METHODS OF CM'S
ESTIMATING FORMATS TOGETHER WITH CM'S AUTOMATED CONSTRUCTION
RESOURCE INFORMATION SYSTEM ON INTERFACING WEIGHTS, VOLUMES
AND MAN-HOURS OF WORK FOR A PROJECT.   PLUMBING

DEMONSTRATION BUILDING TYPE   380.572. SF AIA EQUIVALENT AREA

		QUANTITY	MATERIAL UNIT	LABOR UNIT	EQUIP/ MISC	TOTAL COST	REMARKS	CONTRACT ELEMENT
EQUIPMENT AND FIXTURES								
7305	DOMESTIC WATER STOR.TANK(STEEL) 1000 GAL	2 EA	2449.95	120.17	143.98	5.428		
7345	HOT WATER GENERATOR (ELECTRIC) 400GPH	3 EA	6309.65	328.54	129.58	20.304		15420
7385	PUMP UNIT WITH CONTROLS PER GPM	75 EA	29.20	6.85	.00	2.703		15420
7400	FLOOR DRAIN W/TRAP - PIPE SIZE 2" TO 3"	28 EA	72.56	40.71	.00	3.172		15420
7410	SHOWER DRAIN W/STRAINER	504 EA	101.00	40.71	.00	71.420		15460
7425	CLEAN OUTS-WALL	40 EA	116.68	18.29	.00	5.399		15460
7426	CLEAN OUTS-FLOOR	62 EA	108.83	29.25	.00	8.561		15065
7437	HOSE BIBBS	6 EA	14.24	8.41	.00	135		15065
7449	WATER CLOSET - WALL HUNG W/FLUSH VALVE	504 EA	212.88	86.52	.00	150.893		15460
7452	WATER CLOSET - WALL HUNG FOR CARRIER ADD	504 EA	157.74	30.53	.00	94.892		15460
7467	LAVATORY-WALL HUNG-VITREOUS CHINA	504 EA	188.54	66.16	.00	128.367		15460
7477	LAVATORY-FOR WALL CARRIERS ADD	504 EA	72.11	25.45	.00	49.169		15460
7494	SINK - MOP RECEPTOR (FLOOR)	6 EA	285.44	96.69	.00	2.293		15460
7524	SHOWER HEAD SET-STANDARD	504 EA	96.89	41.12	.00	69.559		15460
7513	DRINKING FOUNTAIN-ELEC COOLER FULLY RECS	8 EA	1039.32	132.34	.00	9.374		15460
					SUBTOTAL = $	621.669	1.63 PER SF 290.50 PER FIXT	
PIPING AND ACCESSORIES								
7643	PIPING-COPPER TYPE L W/FTGS & HGRS 1/2"	44.646 LF	1.34	2.85	.00	187.051		15065
7644	PIPING-COPPER TYPE L W/FTGS & HGRS 3/4"	59.527 LF	1.86	3.17	.00	299.661		15065
7645	PIPING-COPPER TYPE L W/FTGS & HGRS 1"	31.480 LF	2.57	4.15	.21	218.314		15065
7646	PIPING-COPPER TYPE L W/FTGS & HGRS 11/4"	12.402 LF	3.20	4.61	.21	99.497		15065
7647	PIPING-COPPER TYPE L W/FTGS & HGRS 11/2"	24.803 LF	4.31	5.30	.21	243.743		15065
7648	PIPING-COPPER TYPE L W/FTGS & HGRS 2"	18.615 LF	6.43	5.54	.21	226.751		15065
7696	PIPING - CAST IRON W/FTGS UNDERGRND 4"	24.803 LF	5.44	6.00	.62	299.967		15065
7701	PIPING - CAST IRON W/FTGS UNDERGRND 10"	899 LF	22.14	14.57	.82	33.740		15065
7709	PIPING-CAST IRON W/FTG & HGR NO-HUB 2"	20.695 LF	3.05	4.49	.21	160.350		15065
7710	PIPING-CAST IRON W/FTG & HGR NO-HUB 3"	15.502 LF	3.64	4.81	.38	136.707		15065
7711	PIPING-CAST IRON W/FTG & HGR NO-HUB 4"	22.323 LF	5.02	5.30	.60	243.908		15065

Figure 4-18 Quantity takeoff.

tities of material needed for the project are recorded on computer cards.

The result is a deck of computer cards that represent the quantities and types of materials needed for the building. The fact that the quantity takeoff is stored on separate cards makes changing or updating the estimate easy, since the estimator can pull only those cards affected by design changes rather than revising the entire estimate or the unit-cost file each time.

The computer processes each card, retrieves the materials' descriptions and unit costs, makes the necessary calculations, and prints the materials estimate. It can sort costs into many categories and summaries. Even when a project is in the schematic-design phase we can produce a quantity takeoff; and the takeoff might need to be updated periodically to reflect changes in the needs for certain materials as the building's design is finalized. Perhaps by the end of design development the quantity of 2-inch type L copper piping required will differ from what was predicted during schematic design. The estimating team will be able to keep the takeoff current by pulling and revising just the 2-inch type L copper piping card.

The quantity takeoff details how much of the material will be needed; the total cost of the installed material; and breakdowns of the prices by material cost, labor cost, and equipment cost per unit. On the printout in Figure 4-18, we see that the current design for this megaproject calls for 18,615 linear feet of 2-inch type L copper piping, and that we'll be paying approximately $6.50 per linear foot (a *unit*) for materials, $5.50 for labor, and 21 cents for equipment—a total of $226,751 for all of the 2-inch type L copper piping involved in this project. If the price changed tomorrow, we could update the proper card and know the ramifications within 30 minutes.

The fourth source of input for the estimating program is the resource file (see Figure 4-19). The resource file lists

```
CM INC., CONSTRUCTORS/MANAGERS     DEMONSTRATION BUILDING TYPE
COST CONTROL SYSTEM     SCHEMATIC DESIGN                                    RESOURCES CSI FORMAT    PAGE: 16
                                                                                              CM TAKE-OFF DETAIL
*****************************************************************************************************************
                                                                   TOTAL     SHIPPING    SHIPPING      MAN
CSI SECTION     CM ITEM DESCRIPTION                    QUANTITY      COST      WEIGHT      VOLUME       HOURS
*****************************************************************************************************************
                                                                               LB          CF          HR

DIVISION 15  -  MECHANICAL                (CONTINUED)
------------------------------------------------------------------
    15060   MECHANICAL PIPING             (CONTINUED)
------------------------------------------------------------------
     5844   HEATING SPECIALTIES-TRAPS,VALVES&FITNGS      LS     5.398                 .00       61.23
     5846   HEATING SPECIALTIES-HOT WATER SYSTEM         LS     2.921                 .00       33.14
     5890   PIPING SPECIALTIES                           LS     7.057                 .00      115.19
     5605   PIPING-COPPER TYPE K(ACR)W/FTG&HGR   1"    5984 LF  53.573     5.984     41.89    1,469.38
     5607   PIPING-COPPER TYPE K(ACR)W/FTG&HGR 11/2"   3989 LF  51.807     5.983     63.82    1,212.93
     5577   MECHANICAL PIPING(WELDED)     3 IN BLACK   9078 LF 110.140    75.347    771.63    2,730.56
     5577   MECHANICAL PIPING(WELDED)     3 IN BLACK   9245 LF 112.171    76.733    785.82    2,780.79
     5850   VALVES AND FITTINGS                          LS    72.574                 .00      758.28
     5890   PIPING SPECIALTIES                           LS    42.956                 .00      701.25
     597A   WATER CCIL PIPING HOOK UP W/RR.LINE11/2"    9 EA     6.411      351     18.72       54.04
     5976   WATER CCIL PIPING HOOK UP W/RR.LINE11/2"   12 EA     8.548      468     24.96       72.05
                                                                --------------------------------------------
                                                     SUBTOTAL  722.951   261.559   3,483.61   12,515.92

    15065   PLUMBING PIPING
            --------------
     7425   CLEAN OUTS-WALL                            40 EA     5.399       80      4.00       36.87
     7426   CLEAN OUTS-FLOOR                           62 EA     8.561      124      6.20       91.40
     7643   PIPING-COPPER TYPE L W/FTGS & HGRS   1/2" 44646 LF 187.051    15.626   133.94    6,418.50
     7644   PIPING-COPPER TYPE L W/FTGS & HGRS   3/4" 59527 LF 299.661    30.359   238.11    9,513.35
     7645   PIPING-COPPER TYPE L W/FTGS & HGRS   1"   31480 LF 218.314    26.758   220.36    6,590.83
     7646   PIPING-COPPER TYPE L W/FTGS & HGRS 11/4"  12402 LF  99.497    12.650   124.02    2,882.17
     7647   PIPING-COPPER TYPE L W/FTGS & HGRS 11/2"  24803 LF 243.743    32.244   396.84    6,629.60
     7648   PIPING-COPPER TYPE L W/FTGS & HGRS   2"   18615 LF 226.751    37.230   577.06    5,196.45
     769A   PIPING - CAST IRON W/FTGS UNDERGRND   4"  24803 LF 298.967   409.249  3,968.48   7,495.08
     7701   PIPING - CAST IRON W/FTGS UNDERGRND  10"    899 LF  33.740    44.950   773.14      660.02
     7709   PIPING-CAST IRON W/FTG & HGR NO-HUB    2"  20695 LF 160.350    95.197   827.80    4,679.45
     7710   PIPING-CAST IRON W/FTG & HGR NO-HUB    3"  15502 LF 136.707    97.663  1,705.22   3,754.06
     7711   PIPING-CAST IRON W/FTG & HGR NO-HUB    4"  22323 LF 243.908   196.442  3,571.68   5,966.72
     7713   PIPING-CAST IRON W/FTG & HGR NO-HUB    6"   4101 LF  67.059    61.515  1,353.33   1,493.98
     7714   PIPING-CAST IRON W/FTG & HGR NO-HUB    8"   2467 LF  67.788    56.741  1,406.19   1,394.56
     7803   VALVES                                       LS    79.813                 .00      905.39
     7711   PIPING-CAST IRON W/FTG & HGR NO-HUB    4"    630 LF   6.883     5.544   100.80      168.39
                                                                --------------------------------------------
                                                     SUBTOTAL 2,384.192  1,122.372 15,407.18  63,876.83

    15180   INSULATION - MECHANICAL
     5655   INSUL.FIBER GLASS-  1IN-PIPE SIZE   1IN    9A LF     411       39      5.88       11.56
     5658   INSUL.FIBER GLASS-  1IN-PIPE SIZE   2IN   676 LF   3.509      541     74.36       92.94
     5662   INSUL.FIBER GLASS-11/2IN-PIPE SIZE  3IN    92 LF     685      120     23.00       15.47
     5663   INSUL.FIBER GLASS-11/2IN-PIPE SIZE  4IN    36 LF     314       61     12.60        6.78
```

Figure 4-19 Resource file.

the shipping weight, shipping volume, and labor needs involved in installing the materials listed in the unit-cost file. The resources are broken into CSI categories, and within these categories, the report first lists the quantity required for the project based on early design drawings and then calculates the costs associated with getting the material in place. The subtotals represent the cost of the total installed system.

In the resource file, as part of the plumbing piping section, the quantity and total cost of 2-inch type L copper piping (from the quantity takeoff) are listed together with the shipping weight (in pounds), the shipping volume (in cubic feet), and the labor hours required to install all 18,615 feet. The subtotals for the sections help us figure what percentage of the total cost each system represents.

Estimating Program

The computer program that produces the estimate is conceptually simple. It retrieves material costs from the unit-cost file, multiplies them by the factors, the quantity takeoff, and the resource file results, and prints out the cumulative numbers. The program's power lies in its flexibility and its large data-handling capacity.

Good support for a design effort lies in pricing many alternatives and testing many design directions early in a project. A good estimating system must keep pace with the imagination of a facile designer, so design must be quickly translated into cost. And while most estimating systems are developed using the most basic elements in construction—bricks, plumbing fixtures, conduit, reinforced steel, etc.—our program allows us to combine these elements into logically organized groups, components, and modules to expedite the estimating process for analysis of design alternatives.

This enables us to deal efficiently with buildings that are repeated from site to site, as when we are building a series of military installations. We can estimate building types (cafeterias, barracks, teaching facilities, etc.) and adjust costs to reflect any price or size differential between installation locations. Or, if the project is a large housing development, we can estimate by residential room types (kitchen A, B, and C; bedroom 1, 2, and 3; etc.). Then we can store that information and use it as building blocks to design a variety of housing units to meet the project budget.

We can also group concrete with formwork and reinforcing steel to deal with the in-place cost of concrete work. Kitchens and bathrooms can be estimated as "wet core modules." This technique simplifies the estimating of repetitive construction. A construction system can be estimated once, given a descriptive title, and stored in the data bank. Then it can be recalled as often and in as many multiples, combinations, or varieties as required. There's no loss of accuracy using this technique either, because the specific quantities of any material can always be recovered from a wall or enclosure system or the entire project.

We can retrieve information on the cost of 2-inch type L copper piping from the plumbing system, the total cost of bathroom fixtures, the whole bathroom, the whole building, or the whole project. The advantage of the "system" estimating technique lies in its ability to produce quick cost results. In conventional estimating, simple changes might require time-consuming exercises to determine their effects. But with this capability many alternatives can be easily tested.

The program also has the capability of categorizing construction costs into special breakdowns based on the specific needs of a project, provided they are known to the estimator prior to the takeoff. For example, if an owner wants to know the cost of each floor of a high rise, our estimator can arrange to have the to-date cost of each story included in all the estimating reports.

The system can also convert currencies and measurement systems. If we are working on an overseas job but buying the construction materials in the United States, our system can print the estimate in both dollars and the currency of the country where the project is being built. Or we can take off materials in feet and inches, retrieve data in dollars and cents, and print out results in meters and francs.

Estimating Output

The cost information needed by each project participant differs. The architect needs to see the cost system by

CM SUPPORT SYSTEMS **159**

system in order to decide whether to use concrete or steel structure, rooftop or central HVAC systems, masonry or precast skin. A client needs to know cost per functional area. For instance, the developer may want to compare the cost of the commercial shopping space in a building with the office-rental space. And we, the construction managers, need to know construction prices contract by contract so we can evaluate bids and negotiate contracts.

Our program produces different estimates for these different needs. This flexibility is one of its most attractive features. Each format can be produced in three basic levels of detail, making nine variations in all.

1 *System (or CM) format.* The system format categorizes construction cost by building system. It is mainly used during the design phase to assist the architect-engineer in making design decisions.

The three levels of reports in this format are the project summary, the systems summary, and the detail estimate. The project summary (see Figure 4-20) is

```
CM INC., CONSTRUCTORS/MANAGERS    2700 SOUTH POST OAK ROAD, SUITE 2200   HOUSTON, TEXAS 77056    (713) 622-5030        01 NOV 79
COST CONTROL SYSTEM          ESTIMATOR: BYRON STENIS                                           CM FORMAT    PAGE:   1

DEMONSTRATION PROJECT                          HOUSTON, TEXAS
SCHEMATIC DESIGN
                                                                                               PROJECT SUMMARY
THIS ESTIMATE WILL INDICATE VARIOUS METHODS OF CM'S
ESTIMATING FORMATS TOGETHER WITH CM'S AUTOMATED CONSTRUCTION
RESOURCE INFORMATION SYSTEM ON INTERFACING WEIGHTS, VOLUMES
AND MAN-HOURS OF WORK FOR A PROJECT.

DEMONSTRATION BUILDING TYPE                                                 380,572. SF AIA EQUIVALENT AREA

••••••••••••••••••••••••••••••••••••••••••••••••••••••••••••••••••••••••••••••••••••••••••••••••••••••••••••••••••••••

          A  CONSTRUCTION COST

             1  BUILDING COST

                ARCHITECTURAL         26.03/SF          9,907,138.00     37.0% OF  A1

                STRUCTURAL            18.70/SF          7,117,627.00     26.6% OF  A1

                MECHANICAL             9.63/SF          3,663,342.00     13.7% OF  A1

                PLUMBING               9.21/SF          3,505,884.00     13.1% OF  A1

                ELECTRICAL             5.46/SF          2,077,263.00      7.8% OF  A1

                CONVEYING SYSTEM       1.26/SF            480,394.00      1.8% OF  A1
                                                    ----------------
                TOTAL BUILDING COST  $ 70.29/SF  $    26,751,648.00

             2  FIXED EQUIPMENT                    $       608,141.00      2.3% OF  A1

             3  SITE DEVELOPMENT                   $     1,120,578.00      4.2% OF  A1
                                                    ================
                TOTAL CONSTRUCTION COST            $    28,480,367.00
                                                    ================
       TOTAL PROJECT COST                          $    28,480,367.00
```

Figure 4-20 Project summary.

divided into the traditional building disciplines—architectural, structural, mechanical, plumbing, electrical, and conveying—which constitute the building cost. For each discipline, the project summary provides the cost per unit, the total cost, and the percentage of the building cost each fraction represents.

Fixed equipment and site development are listed separately and combined with the building cost to give the total project cost. Their prices are shown in relation to the building cost.

The systems summary gives the relative cost of building systems for each building discipline, broken into labor, material, and equipment costs. The detail estimate is an item-by-item listing of every item in the estimate—from steel beams to doorknobs. It records quantity and material, labor, and equipment costs.

2   *CSI format.* The CSI format categorizes construction cost by Construction Specifications Institute divisions. It is used to identify costs by trade and to help in devising bid strategies. Within the CSI format the three levels of reporting are the division summary, the section summary, and the takeoff detail.

The division summary (see Figure 4-21) shows the sixteen CSI divisions, with totals for material, labor, and equipment for each division. The section summary breaks down each CSI division into its subsets, giving material, labor, and equipment costs.

3   *Contract format.* The contract format categorizes construction cost by potential contract. It strategizes how the construction managers will want to bid and build a project. It regroups the CSI divisions into contracts with option totals by bid packages, ranked ac-

```
CM ASSOCIATES, INC.    2700 SOUTH POST OAK ROAD, SUITE 2200   HOUSTON, TEXAS 77056   (713) 622-5030                              28 JUN 77
COST CONTROL SYSTEM               ESTIMATOR: BYRON STENIS                                            CSI FORMAT   PAGE:    1

DEMONSTRATION PROJECT                        HOUSTON, TEXAS                          JUL 77 MID-CONSTRUCTION DATE
SCHEMATIC DESIGN                                                          BASED ON INFORMATION AVAILABLE 15 MAY 77
                                                                                            CSI DIVISION SUMMARY
THIS ESTIMATE WILL INDICATE VARIOUS METHODS OF CM'S
ESTIMATING FORMATS TOGETHER WITH CM'S AUTOMATED CONSTRUCTION
RESOURCE INFORMATION SYSTEM ON INTERFACING WEIGHTS, VOLUMES
AND MAN-HOURS FOR A PROJECT.

DORMITORY                                                                380,572. SF AIA EQUIVALENT AREA

                                             MATERIAL        LABOR          OTHER          TOTAL
                                               COST           COST           COST           COST

       DIVISION 01  -  GENERAL CONDITIONS         14,216       76,629         27,325        118,170
       DIVISION 02  -  SITE WORK                 461,629      317,945         86,285        865,859
       DIVISION 03  -  CONCRETE                3,699,676    2,304,488        306,705      6,310,869
       DIVISION 04  -  MASONRY                   393,189      702,746         69,695      1,165,630
       DIVISION 05  -  METALS                     97,611       39,479          3,639        140,729
       DIVISION 06  -  WOOD AND PLASTIC          414,179      207,624          4,555        626,358
       DIVISION 07  -  THERMAL AND MOISTURE PROTECTION  232,597  165,914       6,652        405,163
       DIVISION 08  -  DOORS AND WINDOWS         806,517      257,577             0       1,064,094
       DIVISION 09  -  FINISHES                  730,736    1,335,315         71,261      2,137,312
       DIVISION 10  -  SPECIALTIES               117,140       41,652             76        158,868
       DIVISION 11  -  EQUIPMENT                 127,228       31,358            270        158,856
       DIVISION 12  -  FURNISHINGS                     0            0              0              0
       DIVISION 13  -  SPECIAL CONSTRUCTION            0            0              0              0
       DIVISION 14  -  CONVEYING SYSTEMS               0            0              0              0
       DIVISION 15  -  MECHANICAL               2,517,177    1,724,627        56,381      4,298,185
       DIVISION 16  -  ELECTRICAL                739,379      767,983              0      1,507,362
                                              10,351,274    7,973,337        632,844     18,957,455
```

Figure 4-21   CSI division summary.

cording to bidding priority. The three reports are the contract summary, the contract elements summary, and the contract detail summary.

The contract summary (illustrated in Figure 4-22) lists various bid packages together with a shopping list of contract bid items that make up each package. Costs for material, labor, and equipment and a total for each contract bid are listed with the appropriate bid package. The contract elements summary breaks down each bid package into its components, giving material, labor, equipment, and total cost for each element of the bid package. The contract detail estimate further defines the bid package elements, giving for each specific item of the contract bid package the quantity and the material, labor, and equipment costs, as well as a total cost for each item.

```
CM INC., CONSTRUCTORS/MANAGERS     2700 SOUTH POST OAK ROAD, SUITE 2200    HOUSTON, TEXAS 77056    (713) 622-5030        01 NOV 79
COST CONTROL SYSTEM                   ESTIMATOR: BYRON STENIS                                       CONTRACT FORMAT    PAGE:   1

DEMONSTRATION PROJECT                        HOUSTON, TEXAS
SCHEMATIC DESIGN
                                                                                                        CONTRACT SUMMARY
THIS ESTIMATE WILL INDICATE VARIOUS METHODS OF CM'S
ESTIMATING FORMATS TOGETHER WITH CM'S AUTOMATED CONSTRUCTION
RESOURCE INFORMATION SYSTEM ON INTERFACING WEIGHTS, VOLUMES
AND MAN-HOURS OF WORK FOR A PROJECT.

DEMONSTRATION BUILDING TYPE                                                   380,572. SF AIA EQUIVALENT AREA
•••••••••••••••••••••••••••••••••••••••••••••••••••••••••••••••••••••••••••••••••••••••••••••••••••••••••••••••
       CONTRACT    CM                                               MATERIAL    LABOR    OTHER      TOTAL
       ELEMENT   ITEM   DESCRIPTION                      QUANTITY      COST      COST     COST       COST    REMARKS
•••••••••••••••••••••••••••••••••••••••••••••••••••••••••••••••••••••••••••••••••••••••••••••••••••••••••••••••

         A       BID PACKAGE A
        --------------------------------------------------------------------
         A   -   1 PRE-PURCHASE MECHANICAL EQUIPMENT        942,486         0          0      942,486
         A   -   2 PRE-PURCHASE PLUMBING EQUIPMENT           28,469         0          0       28,469
         A   -   3 PRE-PURCHASE ELECTRICAL SECONDARY POWER  450,812         0          0      450,812
                                                         -----------  ---------  --------  -----------
                                                         1,421,767         0          0    1,421,767

         B       BID PACKAGE B
        --------------------------------------------------------------------
         B   -   1 BUILDING EXCAVATION AND EARTHWORK         38,435   168,598     89,360      296,393
         B   -   2 REINFORCED AND PRECAST CONCRETE        5,499,883 3,318,995    312,020    9,130,898
         B   -   3 MISCELLANEOUS IRON AND METALS            134,076    55,943      4,556      194,575
         B   -   4 ROOFING,THERMAL AND MOISTURE PROTECTION  361,241   198,417      5,565      565,223
                                                         ----------- ---------  --------  ------------
                                                         6,033,635 3,741,953    411,501   10,187,089

         C       BID PACKAGE C
        --------------------------------------------------------------------
         C   -   1 MASONRY                                  403,660   690,713     64,168    1,158,541
         C   -   2 LATH AND PLASTER                         459,916 1,372,104     96,009    1,928,029
         C   -   3 CARPENTRY                                166,596   154,115      5,968      326,679
         C   -   4 MECHANICAL                             1,080,399 1,601,033     36,710    2,718,142
```

Figure 4-22   Contract summary.

PROJECT ACCOUNTING

Project accounting systems are designed to monitor the financial standing of projects and report on their financial condition at any stage during their design and construction. Our project accounting system at CM Inc. is computer-based, which enables us to retrieve, update, and refine estimates quickly and accurately, adjusting our figures to reflect current project status in minutes.

Project accounting systems can be set up on an individual basis to report on total project expenditures made to date, the money paid out to a specific contractor, the balance remaining on the architectural fee, or the upcoming month's expenses. Our system produces three basic reports: cost status, payment status, and contract detail status.

Cost status reports present the current and historical cost of the project up to the reporting date. For each contract they list the original budget, the last current working estimate, and the base commitment (awarded contract amount) for any given contract item. The cost of approved change orders for a contract added to the base commitment gives the total commitment. This total combined with pending change orders shows the total estimated cost to complete. The report also provides subtotals for the cost status of the bid packages.

In addition to the committed and potential cost of the contract, the cost status report flags two important comparisons:

1 It shows how closely the estimate and the base commitment coincide. This comparison is called the *variance* and in some cases alerts the project team to the fact that additional funds might be needed.

2 It shows how the client's budget compares with the total estimated cost to complete—in other words, how much the budget has changed. This plainly spells out whether a contract is within range.

In Figure 4-23, in bid package B, we can see that item number 2, reinforcement and precast concrete, was budgeted at $8,504,700 but the last estimate shows it at $8,211,748—a difference of minus $292,952. The cost of awarded work ($8,163,343) plus the cost of approved change orders ($43,173) and pending change orders ($12,364) puts the current estimate to complete at $8,218,880—a figure which is higher than the last estimate but still $285,820 below the budget allocation.

The *payment status report* (Figure 4-24) shows the contract work in progress in both dollars and percentage completed, and the amount of money owed for that work, minus the client's retainage. The program calculates the percentage completed, which represents the value of work in place divided by the total commitment.

	BUDGET ALLOCATION (A)	ESTIMATE (B)	DIFFERENCE (C=B-A)	BASE COMMITMENT (D)	VARIANCE (E=D-B)	APPRV C. O. (F)	TOTAL COMMITMENT (G=D+F)	PENDING C.O. (H)	EST COST COMPLETE (I=G+H)	CHG FROM BUDGET (J=I-A) *OR(I=B)
CONSTRUCTION										
BID PACKAGE A										
1. PRE-PURCHASE MECH EQUIP	810,998	810,998	0	778,558	32,440-	0	778,558	0	778,558	32,440-
2. PRE-PURCHASE PLUMB EQUI	30,700	27,119	3,581-	28,746	1,627	0	28,746	0	28,746	1,954-
3. PRE-PURCHASE ELECT EQUI	275,300	266,426	8,874-	253,105	13,321-	0	253,105	0	253,105	22,195-
TOTAL	1,116,998	1,104,543	12,455-	1,060,409	44,134-	0	1,060,409	0	1,060,409	56,589-
BID PACKAGE B										
1. EXCAVATION & EARTHWORK	267,500	275,423	7,923	268,167	7,256-	15,961	284,128	0	284,128	16,628
2. REINF & PRECAST CONCRET	8,504,700	8,211,748	292,952-	8,163,343	48,405-	43,173	8,206,516	12,364	8,218,880	285,820-
3. MISC IRON AND METALS	185,400	180,647	4,753-	0	N/A	N/A	0	N/A	180,647	4,753-
4. ROOFING/THERMAL/MOISTUR	535,900	537,737	1,837	0	N/A	N/A	0	N/A	537,737	1,837
TOTAL	9,493,500	9,205,555	287,945-	8,431,510	55,661-	59,134	8,490,644	12,364	9,221,392	272,108-
BID PACKAGE C										
1. MASONRY	1,153,600	1,107,874	45,726-	0	N/A	N/A	0	N/A	1,107,874	45,726-
2. LATH AND PLASTER	1,750,400	1,696,303	54,097-	0	N/A	N/A	0	N/A	1,696,303	54,097-
3. CARPENTRY	309,700	311,904	2,204	0	N/A	N/A	0	N/A	311,904	2,204
4. MECHANICAL	2,518,400	2,417,065	101,335-	2,417,065	0	0	2,417,065	0	2,417,065	101,335-
5. PLUMBING	3,227,000	3,198,168	28,832-	3,202,135	3,967	0	3,202,135	0	3,202,135	24,865-
6. ELECTRICAL	1,675,400	1,656,168	19,232-	1,656,168	0	0	1,656,168	0	1,656,168	19,232-
7. CONVEYING SYSTEM	453,700	443,523	10,177-	0	N/A	N/A	0	N/A	443,523	10,177-
TOTAL	11,088,200	10,831,005	257,195-	7,275,368	3,967	0	7,275,368	0	10,834,972	253,228-
BID PACKAGE D										
1. WINDOW WALL & GLAZING	513,600	466,667	46,933-	0	N/A	N/A	0	N/A	466,667	46,933-
2. DOORS/FRAMES/HARDWARE	642,900	625,704	17,196-	0	N/A	N/A	0	N/A	625,704	17,196-
3. CERAMIC TILE	549,300	536,662	12,638-	0	N/A	N/A	0	N/A	536,662	12,638-
4. FLOORING & CARPET	545,900	546,960	1,060	0	N/A	N/A	0	N/A	546,960	1,060
TOTAL	2,251,700	2,175,993	75,707-	0	N/A	N/A	0	N/A	2,175,993	75,707-
BID PACKAGE E										
1. PAINTING	550,000	544,423	5,577-	0	N/A	N/A	0	N/A	544,423	5,577-
2. GENERAL WORKS	885,000	900,895	15,895	0	N/A	N/A	0	N/A	900,895	15,895
TOTAL	1,435,000	1,445,318	10,318	0	N/A	N/A	0	N/A	1,445,318	10,318

Figure 4-23 Cost status report.

	TOTAL COMMITMENT (A)	VALUE IN PLACE BAL FWRD (B)	VALUE IN PLACE CURRENT (C)	(INVOICED) TO DATE (D=B+C)	PCT (D/A)	RETAIN AGE (E)	TOTAL AMOUNT PAYABLE BAL FWRD (F)	TOTAL AMOUNT PAYABLE CURRENT (G=H-F)	TO DATE (H=D-E)	BALANCE ON CONTRACT (I=A-H)
CONSTRUCTION										
BID PACKAGE A										
1. PRE-PURCHASE MECH EQUIP	778,558	778,558	0	778,558	100.0%	77,856	700,702	0	700,702	77,856
2. PRE-PURCHASE PLUMB EQUI	28,746	28,746	0	28,746	100.0%	2,875	25,871	0	25,871	2,875
3. PRE-PURCHASE ELECT EQUI	253,105	253,104	0	253,104	100.0%	25,310	227,794	0	227,794	25,311
TOTAL	1,060,409	1,060,408	0	1,060,408	100.0%	106,041	954,367	0	954,367	106,042
BID PACKAGE B										
1. EXCAVATION & EARTHWORK	284,128	284,126	0	284,126	100.0%	28,413	255,713	0	255,713	28,415
2. REINF & PRECAST CONCRET	8,206,516	3,059,583	0	3,059,583	37.3%	305,958	2,753,625	0	2,753,625	5,452,891
3. MISC IRON AND METALS	0	N/A	N/A	N/A	0.0%	N/A	N/A	N/A	N/A	N/A
4. ROOFING/THERMAL/MOISTUR	0	N/A	N/A	N/A	0.0%	N/A	N/A	N/A	N/A	N/A
TOTAL	8,490,644	3,343,709	0	3,343,709	39.4%	334,371	3,009,338	0	3,009,338	5,481,306
BID PACKAGE C										
1. MASONRY	0	N/A	N/A	N/A	0.0%	N/A	N/A	N/A	N/A	N/A
2. LATH AND PLASTER	0	N/A	N/A	N/A	0.0%	N/A	N/A	N/A	N/A	N/A
3. CARPENTRY	0	N/A	N/A	N/A	0.0%	N/A	N/A	N/A	N/A	N/A
4. MECHANICAL	2,417,065	69,845	0	69,845	2.9%	6,985	62,860	0	62,860	2,354,205
5. PLUMBING	3,202,135	245,367	0	245,367	7.7%	24,537	220,830	0	220,830	2,981,305
6. ELECTRICAL	1,656,168	105,131	0	105,131	6.3%	10,513	94,618	0	94,618	1,561,550
7. CONVEYING SYSTEM	0	N/A	N/A	N/A	0.0%	N/A	N/A	N/A	N/A	N/A
TOTAL	7,275,368	420,343	0	420,343	5.8%	42,035	378,308	0	378,308	6,897,060
BID PACKAGE D										
1. WINDOW WALL & GLAZING	0	N/A	N/A	N/A	0.0%	N/A	N/A	N/A	N/A	N/A
2. DOORS/FRAMES/HARDWARE	0	N/A	N/A	N/A	0.0%	N/A	N/A	N/A	N/A	N/A
3. CERAMIC TILE	0	N/A	N/A	N/A	0.0%	N/A	N/A	N/A	N/A	N/A
4. FLOORING & CARPET	0	N/A	N/A	N/A	0.0%	N/A	N/A	N/A	N/A	N/A
TOTAL	0	N/A	N/A	N/A	0.0%	N/A	N/A	N/A	N/A	N/A
BID PACKAGE E										
1. PAINTING	0	N/A	N/A	N/A	0.0%	N/A	N/A	N/A	N/A	N/A
2. GENERAL WORKS	0	N/A	N/A	N/A	0.0%	N/A	N/A	N/A	N/A	N/A
TOTAL	0	N/A	N/A	N/A	0.0%	N/A	N/A	N/A	N/A	N/A

Figure 4-24 Payment status report.

The retainage, expressed either as a lump sum or as a percentage figure, subtracted from value in place yields the current payable and to-date payable amounts. The difference between the total commitment and the amount payable to date is the balance on the contract. This information is used for monthly project draws.

In Figure 4-24 in bid package C, for example, for the electrical system (item number 6) we have a total commitment of $1,656,168. Of this, $105,131 worth of work has been put in place and invoiced, bringing the contract to 6.3 percent complete. With a $10,513 retainage (10 percent), that leaves $94,618 payable and a balance on the contract of $1,561,550.

The *contract detail status report* (Figure 4-25) shows the complete activity history of every line item in the accounting structure. It includes the budget, estimate, and base commitment figures for every contract line

```
CM PROJECT ACCOUNTING SYSTEM                         DEMONSTRATION  PROJECT
   REPORT DATE:   06 NOV 79                              FOR ACTIVITY THROUGH:   15 NOV 79
 ●●●●●●●●●●●●●●●●●●●●●●●●●●●●●●●●●●●●●●●●●●●●●●●●●●●●●●●●●●●●●●●●●●●●●●●●●●●●●●●●●●●●●●●●●●●●●●●

CONSTRUCTION
  BID PACKAGE B
    1. EXCAVATION & EARTHWORK
                                 BUDGET =     267,500        ESTIMATE =     275,423

COST STATUS
-----------                                       PROPOSED    APPROVED    REJECTED    PENDING
 BASE COMMITMENT                                              268,167
                                                            ----------
 REF:      PROPOSED   DESCRIPTION              APPR/REJ
 -------------------------------------------------------------
   1     28 APR 79   REVISE ENTRANCE           18 MAY 79     15,961      15,961         0       N/A
 --------------------------------------------------------------------------------------------
                           TOTAL CHANGE ORDERS                15,961      15,961         0         0
                                                            ============
                           TOTAL COMMITMENT                   284,128
                                                            ============
PAYMENT STATUS
--------------
              VALUE  IN  PLACE   (INVOICED)           CUMULATIVE            AMOUNT  PAYABLE
                   CURRENT          TO-DATE            RETAINAGE          TO-DATE        CURRENT
 --------------------------------------------------------------------------------------------
 MAY 79        106,523          106,523        10% =    10,652            95,871         95,871
 JUN 79        119,445          225,968        10% =    22,597           203,371        107,500
 JUL 79         58,158          284,126        10% =    28,413           255,713         52,342
           ----------------------------------------------------------------------------------
                              100.0% INVOICED
                                                                       ============
                              BALANCE ON CONTRACT                           28,415
                                                                       ============
                          VALUE REMAINING TO INVOICE                            ?
                                                                       ============
```

Figure 4-25 Contract detail status report.

item. It also gives the entire change-order history. This includes change-order numbers, their description, proposed and approved dates, and the proposed and approved dollar amounts. If a change order is still pending for several months, it's obvious that someone has dropped the ball. With the detail status report at hand, the project manager can prompt the building team to take action.

The report then summarizes the change orders into an approved total and adds this to the base commitment to get the total commitment. Payment history is also included in the detail report, showing the date, the value in place, the retainage, the current amount payable, and the amount payable to date.

Figure 4-25 shows that within bid package B there is an allotted budget of $267,500 and a recent estimate of $275,423 for excavation and earthwork. One change order, to revise the entrance specification, has been approved, adding $15,961 to the current base commitment, bringing the total to $284,128. The work has been invoiced every month since May and is now 100 percent invoiced; all that's left is the retainage on the last block of work.

EXECUTIVE REPORTING SYSTEMS

Construction projects today have grown to scales no one ever dreamed of, and the only reason CM Inc.'s technology has kept pace is because we had a thorough understanding of our own systems and a willingness to package and unpackage our services. We have always been eager to innovate and to commit ourselves to new horizons, and that has stretched our capabilities tremendously. But all we really did—through years of development and experimentation and our innovation with data programming—was to take management concepts that had been proven in the rest of the business world and apply them to construction.

And in spite of all the changes, *control* remains the critical issue and concern of a construction client. Information, and the distribution of it, has become an end product in itself in construction management.

We developed what we call an *executive reporting system* to meet this and the other special needs of large projects. It is a group of summary reports of all the information generated by the systems we have discussed, compiled in one "executive briefing book"—so top-level management can get an accurate, up-to-date picture of a project in capsule form. Because needs vary from one building program to another, the executive reporting system is adapted to the specific characteristics of each program. But in general, executive reporting systems are designed to:

- Highlight key issues that can have significant impact on the overall project

- Provide the client and the manager with a clear view of the vital signs of the project

- Track and document the decision process, focusing attention on outstanding, unresolved issues

- Help measure performance on the project

In our big projects a clear view of the process is especially hard—and especially important—to formulate. A wide-angle focus must be developed to give the project leaders a panoramic view of the work. And as important as this comprehensive view is, it's not enough: sometimes a tiny detail in the project landscape has disastrous potential. So the system must also have the ability to zoom in from its wide-angle view, locate the troublesome detail, and magnify its repercussions.

That is the strength of the detail reports we have always depended on: their backup shows the project team what has gone awry and where, and allows it to try several hypothetical solutions before taking irreversible action.

5

MANAGING
THE
COMPANY

GOALS

We established three simple goals when we started CM Inc.:

1 *Profit*. To make a better rate of profit than is common in the construction management industry.

2 *Performance*. To fulfill our contracts in letter and spirit and to lead the industry to innovation and quality.

3 *Growth*. To provide professional growth for our employees and financial growth for both our stockholders and our employees.

These are good goals, but hardly unique. Most construction management companies—in fact most all companies—have the same goals. The only way to do better than all the other companies with these same ordinary goals is to work harder at them, and to be more effective together as a team.

Profit, of course, is essential—it's the reason business exists. But few people realize that profit is a result of desire as well as vigor and good management. Companies won't produce good profits unless their leaders *want* them to. The first step is enthusiasm for the idea. And while some professionals, at least publicly, find the idea of profit somehow distasteful, they have an obligation to their stockholders and to themselves to produce profits. Successful companies take pride in their ability to make money.

Performance is a company's ability to meet its obligations and follow through on promises. A good reputation means a lot to a professional service company. It not only brings good clients, it brings and keeps good employees and fuels the fire of pride that produces more good performers.

Growth, as a goal, means growth that is well managed. Company growth accelerates careers and stretches people, whose energy and enthusiasm are in turn recycled into more growth. It increases the value of the stockholder's equity, allows promoting people and giving them raises, and inevitably brings more exciting professional challenges.

Satisfying all three goals—profit, performance, and growth—can cause conflict. Explosive growth can jeopardize performance. Too much devotion to a pet project can cut profits. It's tough to balance the goals, but if you do it right they will support one another.

Bill Caudill of CRS said it best: "Profit helps to improve quality, quality helps to stimulate growth, and growth helps to increase profit." The statement makes the relationship seem obvious, but it doesn't make the day-to-day decisions any easier.

The managers of a company are responsible for making this three-point relationship work. It's easy to satisfy one goal at the expense of another; it's harder to run projects that support all three. It has never been easy to make an above-average profit and grow and perform well, but here are some guidelines and concepts that will help.

ORGANIZATION

Throughout my career I have watched managers struggle with the simpleminded relationships that are depicted on organization charts and try to reconcile them with the complexities of individual strengths, human weaknesses, and the diversity of working relationships that people can develop. In a desire to keep a management concept consistent or a chart symmetrical, they push people into inappropriate positions and force incompatible people to work together. Yet, it's no big secret that it's much better to organize around effective people who like one another.

CM Inc.'s greatest successes have been the result of supporting the right people, instead of following a corporate strategy or management theory. The past and future should be viewed as the result of people and their actions—not as the result of organizational theory or an abstraction called management.

Nonetheless a clear need exists in any professional services company for organization and direction. Leaders, by definition, must be organized enough to say where they are going and whom they are going to rely on to take them there. An organization chart can help set company direction by clarifying vague relationships and by establishing levels of authority. To be organized, a company's people must know what the score is all the time, which means using a management information system that works at the corporate, group, and project levels.

Besides project management, four kinds of administrative activities should be reflected in a construction management company's organization:

1 *Administering routine activities:* wage and salary policies, purchasing, recruiting, information management. These activities are ongoing and have predictable needs for staff.

2 *Planning and causing growth and change:* developing new capabilities and creating new organization. The leadership of the company must be responsible for new directions.

3 *Seizing opportunity:* direct promotion, developing new skills, hiring promising employees. Daily routine should be set aside to pursue opportunity when it emerges. These activities traditionally fall into the extracurricular activities of the key leaders, who must have some reserve for this effort.

4 *Reacting to unusual problems:* unhappy clients or employees, bad bids, or slipping schedules. When trouble strikes you should react immediately and with vigor. A couple of times we have neglected an unhappy client who we thought was making unreasonable demands—only to have that unreasonable client fire us. If a valued employee quits, find out why. Although you can rarely prevent it, you may find a legitimate problem with a solution that will prevent more losses.

Most companies and organization charts consider only the administration of routine activities and staff accordingly. Yet seizing opportunities, solving problems, and planning growth are far more important—and much more difficult—tasks. Leaders must reserve capacity for these extra responsibilities.

Most people equate the theory of organizational hierarchy with degree of importance and salary range. The lofty boxes on the organization chart aren't always of greater importance, nor should they necessarily represent more money. Sometimes outstanding performers don't make good managers. It's foolish for a company to kidnap technical or professional skills for a management assignment—especially foolish for a construction management company, which is dependent on technical as well as managerial functions. If estimators and schedulers must move into administrative roles to be recognized and rewarded, the entire company will suffer from the loss of their applied skills. If technical people are given the authority, respect, and rewards they deserve, they will gladly allow others to provide management support.

GROWTH MANAGEMENT

A company's growth is very rewarding for its leaders; it is a return on all the hard work and time they've invested. It usually means increased billings, which directly mean more funds for improving the company and more profit. But growth can also produce many indirect benefits for a company. Because the company is profitable, staff confidence builds. People are rewarded and promoted. The change growth brings can be stimulating, and the challenge it brings can result in amazing creative efforts. But growth can also cause change and change can damage a company by creating stress, conflict, and confusion.

Reorganization can foster insecurity. Under the pressure created by growth, mistakes are made and then questions as to management's competence and intent pop up. Quality can be a casualty. A growing company must add new employees to its staff each year while replacing employees who leave. Staffing a growing company is extremely difficult; it involves many risks and compromises that are especially dangerous in a profession that depends on its people more than anything else.

Ironically, CM Inc.'s years of rapid growth were plagued with conflict because the company leaders agreed on two principles:

- We should staff new projects with experienced personnel.

- We should keep teams together throughout a project.

Believe it or not, we didn't realize that these two strategies are simply incompatible. A company cannot grow and develop new projects without hiring new people and moving experienced ones around. New-hires, who don't know the company's operations or procedures, can't rally the maximum front-end attention and momentum a new project needs. The best compromise is to have the new people step into positions on existing project teams and transfer the experienced people to new projects.

If project managers groom their subordinates properly, there's a choice of either moving the project manager to a new project or promoting the number 2 person to the number 1 slot. That still breaks up the team, but at least it allows a choice. So staff projects with experienced leaders, but also make sure that the junior project employees have leadership potential. It's also very, very critical to establish a senior officer at the beginning of the project to provide continuity with the client when the project team changes.

Obviously, a construction management company needs people who work hard. And the chance to increase responsibility, authority, and income should provide incentives for hard workers. But in order to deliver on its promises for promotion, a company has to grow. So we have this cycle: Hard work means growth, growth means advancement, advancement means more hard work and more growth. With care a company can capitalize on the benefits of growth and minimize the growing pains. These pointers should help.

1 *Organize for growth.* If the officers are managing, not doing, then they're available to initiate a project and to provide security to the client when staff changes are necessary. A no-growth company can operate with lots of privates and just a few brass, but a growth company is starved for leaders. Hire people with leadership potential. Not everyone will become a leader, or will even want to, but the more people you have to choose from, the better it is for the company.

2 *Evaluate people on results.* At first you must judge people on style, talk, dress, apparent intelligence, values, ethics, and the effort they put into their work—on input, rather than output. But eventually you can evaluate their long-term results—such as the quality of their work, their ability to build a team, and your clients' reactions to them.

Lazy, dishonest, and incompetent people are rarely a threat to a company. They will be found out and fired. The dangerous people are those nice people who have been around for a while doing a mediocre job but developing warm friendships throughout the company; they fill up a slot that an outstanding future leader might hold.

3 *Hire good people when they appear so they'll be there when you need them.* It's a big mistake to wait until you need a new team to start recruiting; the results are anxiety, compromise, and a rough start for a project. But most companies can't afford to inventory people

like office supplies, and good people need an initial challenge to build credibility in the company. Someone who is hired without an immediate project assignment deserves an important nonproject assignment and constant feedback and direction. An entry position may last 6 months; a career is 40 years. Hire for the company, not for the job.

Home-office trial periods are a good way to see how new people function before they are sent on a lead field position. You can make sure they measure up to your impressions and expectations. New employees also need to learn what skills your company can bring to bear on their future projects. And since a service company's skills come in the form of people, new employees need to develop the key personal relationships that are necessary to get action.

4 *Take little jobs along with the big ones.* Big jobs create big profits. They're stimulating; they challenge an organization and force it to constantly adjust its operations to their grand scale. They sponsor development in services and systems that can be applied to other work. They bolster a company's image.

But big jobs can also make a company conservative, by creating overhead and a bureaucracy that cuts into the profitability of the small staple jobs. Also, once a new process is developed for a big job, the natural tendency is to want to apply it to projects that really don't need and can't afford it.

Little jobs keep a company lean and give it staying power. They fill the profit valley between big jobs, so a company with several little jobs is apt to be more stable than one with a few large projects. Since small jobs get done quickly, they are good training ground for managers and possibly the first taste of blood for a promoter. And one way to get big is to find a way to handle a lot of small, profitable projects.

Since a small job may not hold any significant financial incentive, it's necessary to make sure it is strengthening to the firm in some other way. Sometimes it's possible to be more innovative on little jobs, and those innovations can be the cornerstone of future practice. But small jobs require equal attention: a bad reference from a small project hurts as much as a bad reference from a big one.

5 *Make people grow.* CM Inc. grew 40 percent annually throughout the 1970s. At this rate of growth we don't offer people opportunity—we stuff it down their throats. But even companies with less dramatic growth rates must actively present people with the chance to advance and encourage them to take advantage of it. One of our group vice presidents had this line in his annual goals: "My first job is to develop people." There often isn't time to wait until people are fully qualified before you promote them, although the transition period will probably require some judgment. After giving someone a promotion, watch carefully to make sure what you're seeing is stretching, not splitting.

The Peter Principle has an inverse: if people do a good job, their supervisors may want to keep them doing it. An appreciative boss can be a roadblock to staff growth. It's the job of management to identify people with potential and move them up as fast as they can handle it. A person with the potential for rapid growth usually exhibits some of these qualities:

• Is responsible for the *intent* of the work, exceeding average production in both volume and quality

- Is bright and articulate, friendly and open, innovative and communicative

- Is adaptable, a team player who can support not only leaders, but also peers and subordinates

- Works hard, with enthusiasm and a desire to produce the exceptional result

- Respects the company goals and shares the company leaders' values

But this is a boy scout creed, and few people measure up. It's just as likely that a top performer will be an egomaniac driven by self-interest or have an abrasive personality and an inferiority complex. Perfect employees are hard to come by. Often people with great strengths have great weaknesses too. To get the most out of people, employers have to be tolerant and learn to integrate strengths and cover for weaknesses.

6 *Delegate.* Managing your own growth is harder than managing the growth of others. The problem for most people is learning to delegate. The most common mistake is failing to support the delegated effort—then everyone is frustrated and the cycle begins again. The performance of managers should be measured not by what they do, but by the quality of the people they hire and how successful *they* become.

We once hired a management consultant who told us, "Delegate the urgent and deal with the important." Important things having to do with the growth, innovation, and promotion of a company's future can be easily delayed by problems with urgent external deadlines. If the urgent is allowed to take precedence over the important, the managers become controlled by events rather than goals. Managers' individual goals should set the direction for actions; anything extraneous to the goals should be assigned to others.

7 *Assign territories and turn the performers loose.* There is a time to give some special people a territory, either geographical or functional, and with it the autonomy to manage their own efforts. Your relationship will change at this point. Instead of delegating to these people, you offer them counsel and support.

In our early years I participated in every decision at CM Inc. Later, group vice presidents developed all the authority that I once had: they hire and fire, sell work, reassign work, commit the company, and administer salaries. This arrangement is much more than delegation: it's territoriality; and it's a great concept for the continued growth of a company.

8 *Make the parts answer to the whole.* This great concept, decentralization at the decision-making level, requires strong leadership, a clear statement of company goals, and an ideological consensus. It takes leaders who will work for the company goals while tending to the success of their own territory.

But leaders can be tempted to put their own groups' interests first. Some high-performance leaders will resist using company resources, citing the company's imperfections, and in the name of quality, performance, or independence will try to show that they can do it better alone. Even if they succeed, their value to the company decreases because they neither strengthen the company nor gain strength from it.

The trick of good management is to provide order, to sell and perform using the total company forces, to support individuals with the resources of the entire company, and still to provide performers—performers who will help each other because of good will and statesmanship—with room to grow. Their success contributes to the success of the whole company.

SALARY MANAGEMENT

People are a construction management company's greatest asset; salaries are its greatest expense. Matching them proportionately is the greatest challenge and frustration managers face. There are so many complications—between personalities, emotions, economics, negotiations, and inflation. Some examples:

- We all value our own contributions more than anyone else does; thus we all feel underpaid.

- Evaluating people quantitatively is impossible. Personalities and production interfere, and the fact is some people are just plain *worth* more in their position than someone else.

- Different companies pay different salaries, and some will always pay more than you do.

- It's not uncommon in the sporadic construction business to hire people for more than they are worth at critical moments in the company's development. Unfortunately it's only an upward spiral; the people making more than they should will never admit it, and the others see the higher salary as the fair standard.

- Some people who have just been paid a premium to join another company will leak their new salary to their old colleagues before they leave. Rumblings of discontent increase.

The first thing a manager must realize is that there *are* inequities within a company. The economy, company growth, major projects, mistakes in hiring, changes in the industry—all can destroy a methodical approach to compensation. Someone can join a company at a fair salary, do a good job, get promoted, and be compensated at a decent rate of increase. Then a big project comes along and the company must hire people quickly, probably at a premium. There is an explosive situation: the untested new-hire is working alongside a valued employee with seniority—and the recruit is paid more.

So, given the fact that inequities will exist, a wise manager will make sure there are mechanisms to adjust. Of course, you can't average some salaries up and some down—raises are the only real means available. But any company would go broke if it "standardized" everyone up each time a disparity emerged.

The solution is time—with time, individual inequities can be worked out by using promotions, bonuses, and routine salary reviews. Usually an annual review is frequent enough for meaningful evaluation, but your people should be confident that you will treat them well in the long run.

We have developed several salary-management policies that work.

1 *Review salaries in large groups annually.* The large group increases objectivity, and the annual review eliminates impulsive rewards. But each employee should be evaluated individually as well; group raises are an insult to everyone.

This annual schedule should be upset only for truly special cases, such as a substantial increase in responsibility or unexpected performance in a new employee. The best way to stimulate interest for the more ambitious people is to make room for them at the top of the company. If it's true, you can emphasize to these people (and these are probably the people you want to keep) that you're a growth company. Thus performers have a better future with you than with most firms. With that understanding it's easier to keep good people between annual reviews.

Last-ditch attempts to keep valuable people are usually failures, laden with risk. When one company bids against another company to keep someone, it inadvertently encourages people to auction themselves. It would be a bad sign if employment agencies and competitors were to stop poaching your ground, but make sure everyone knows what the headhunters are up to and how often those big front-end salary increases mean disappointing raises down the line.

2 *Pay the fair price.* A company wants to attract people for reasons other than salary. An attractive company—with good people, good projects, good growth—shouldn't have to pay a premium. And the most important argument for hiring at the right salary is that it allows for encouraging raises. The chance to earn a high salary is a strong motivation, but combine this possibility with a chance for responsibility, recognition, self-respect, accomplishment, healthy competition, and leadership and you are offering what every comer is looking for.

It's easy to rationalize paying too much for a reimbursable position on a project, but the figure will always leak out. Then other people, including the client, will feel mistreated, and at the end of the job you'll have an overpaid employee who will be hard to transfer.

It's as bad to pay too little as too much. Low salaries discourage people; their productivity suffers and company morale plummets. And while looking for a bargain in the marketplace, it's tempting to consider people who will hire on for less than they are worth. But to take advantage of them is unfair, and it's bad business. It will be a matter of time before you'll lose them to another company that offers more. Training people is expensive, and profits suffer when a company's continuity is interrupted by personnel turnover.

3 *Compensate quid pro quo.* Rewards should reflect the nature of the job. A routine production job should have routine income; profit sharing should be restricted to people with profit and loss responsibility. This concept does not imply that one type of responsibility is automatically more valuable than the other. Sometimes a person with sophisticated technical abilities will have no control over profits and yet earn more than the combined salary and profit-based bonus of a manager.

It's dangerous to disguise compensation as a gift or make someone feel grateful for a bonus or a raise. People earn their money. Establishing a cause-effect relationship between production and payroll benefits both the employee and the company. If you make people believe that bonuses are gifts of goodwill rather than fair compensation, you will produce apple polishers rather than hard workers.

4 *Have a wide range of raises.* There should be some slight and some significant raises that consider not only what a person's percentage of increase should be but also that person's worth to the company. Here are some basic categories.

Routine raises. A person who stays at the same job and shows no increase in productivity merits a salary increase on an equal rate with inflation. A company that promotes people from the bottom should have a minimum of these types of raises and these types of people.

Performance raises. Some people maintain the same level of responsibility for a long time, but their work becomes better and more productive. They deserve good raises.

Promotion raises. When new responsibilities are assigned, consider an out-of-sequence raise. Titles, such as senior manager, officer, or associate, should be delayed until the person demonstrably measures up to the new job. New titles should offer fringe benefits (such as profit sharing) as well as an opportunity to move up to the next pay scale.

Spectacular raises. If you fail to reward exceptional promise, chances are the person showing it will find someone who will. A spectacular increase is warranted not by a sudden burst of energy or an isolated instance of success but by consistently outstanding performance. It's usually best to wait until the review date. And you should always point out the special nature of the increase so the recipient doesn't think it's standard for the industry.

5 *Manage the average as well as the individual.* Salaries are to a service company what the cost of raw materials is to industry. As every business executive knows, the cost of the raw materials (in this case the average salary) must be tied to the industry's rate of inflation. Most companies equate the inflation rate with the consumer price index (CPI), but that can't mean individual raises must be limited to the

CPI. As a company grows, people are promoted, and new people start at entry-level salaries. This low end of the spectrum dilutes the average overall salary; hence the possibility of substantial raises for good performers.

The CPI isn't infallible; it's used because there may be nothing else. There are periods of unusual inflation rates in special job categories that can't be measured or predicted. The manager of a construction management company will learn about those conditions just by being in the market, and firsthand knowledge of current conditions must augment the CPI guidelines. If there were a good index of salary inflation for the construction management industry, you'd want to use that.

6 *Give raises on time.* If people are told when they are going to be reviewed, they are justified in getting upset when the date slips. That takes most of the value out of the raise.

7 *Trust young people.* Heap on the work and responsibility, then help them deliver. As duties increase, their salaries can be worked out to total more than the going rate for their age and experience level, but less than their position might command. That's a good deal for everyone.

Surprisingly enough, a manager often has to encourage young people to trust other young people. Men and women rapidly promoted to leadership positions are the first to mistrust inexperience and seek out seasoned veterans for their teams.

8 *Exploit the prejudices of others.* Some of the best values in the employment marketplace are people who, for reasons of prejudice, are rejected else-

where. Sexism, racism, and ageism are not only against the law, they're dumb. There are also less blatant prejudices to watch for in the construction industry. You can benefit from the fact that many construction management companies recognize neither the competence of youth and women nor the value of education.

9 *Review salaries only in formal situations.* One of the most uncomfortable flights a manager can take is trapped in a window seat next to an employee who feels underpaid. If this situation arises, there's only one logical response, and that is to say and do nothing. To avoid the situation you must convey to your people that much formal thought, planning, and rationale go into salary reviews and demonstrate that action, not argument, warrants a raise.

10 *Grow the company from the bottom.* There is a natural tendency to hire people who are fully trained for job openings. But that minimizes the chance for promotions, and again, career potential should be one of the benefits a company offers good people to supplement their salaries. This "grow from the bottom" concept depends on company leaders who will devote time to teaching employees and grooming them for promotion.

The conceptual weakness is that you can only teach and groom in areas where you are qualified—if you want new capabilities you must add specialists at higher levels. Then they train people in their fields. To grow from the bottom a company must have great teachers *and* great recruiters.

11 *Double the effort on international compensation.* As difficult as it is to manage domestic salaries, it's twice as tough overseas, where things can be four times as

expensive. It's essential to have up-to-the-minute market information on international rates—otherwise you'll alienate your good people and miss out on some new ones.

EXPENSE MANAGEMENT

One of the things a manager must learn right away is how to say no to a request for something an employee thinks would be "nice." It probably *would* be nice, and no boss wants to be seen as a ruthless taskmaster, depriving employees in the name of productivity. But money should be spent only on essentials: on things that will save money or make money and on investments in growth.

Expenses are controlled by a combination of attitudes, policies, and rules. Attitudes work better than policies, and policies work better than rules. To a company this means that (1) the right attitudes need to be communicated and (2) responsible people are needed to make their attitude-based management system successful.

Direct job expenses, particularly travel, are most effectively controlled with attitude management. Most companies have lenient travel expense policies that assume people will be judicious. But people need to know that a company wants them to save money, and they need to know what constitutes an appropriate expense. A company must set the tone and supply some guidelines for people to base their judgment on.

If expenses aren't checked periodically to monitor poor judgment, they will grow continuously. The right and wrong attitudes are evident in all the little things—the cars people rent, the hotels and restaurants they choose, the way they tip. Some people make three copies when they need two, use air freight when parcel post would do, write lengthy telexes, and chat on long-distance phone calls. Some team up for travel when they could really go it alone, and that wastes time as well as money.

Foreign work expenses usually need more control than attitudes alone can offer. Defined policies are needed in high-cost foreign environments where the cost of renting personnel housing may exceed the entire fee on a $10 million domestic job. Rules usually crop up when some liberty has been used to advantage; they're an arbitrary and stingy way to control expenses.

But to make money, you've got to know your income and your expenses and make the tough decisions early enough to keep expense below income. Our experience has shown that the only intelligent income and expense projections are built up from the project level. Statistical projections are unreliable. It's dangerous to rationalize that operations will be supported by *potential* sales that may or may not materialize. You must develop contingency plans that ensure profits based on real, contracted scheduled billings.

A surefire way to financial disaster is to delegate authority to spend money without attaching equal accountability. Expenses can be controlled only by responsible people through a combination of expense decentralization and accountability. Cost management is a responsibility for people who can evaluate and control costs within a certain level—project managers and their project costs, group vice presidents and group overhead, corporate management and corporate overhead, etc. Regular reports, generated at all levels, complete the system of checks and balances. They're the only way to keep up with a company's expenses.

Expense managment is not only an internal issue. It affects outside relationships as well. A construction management organization must be careful to execute the exact services stipulated in each contract—no more, no less. Clients don't usually appreciate freebies (they're usually suspicious of them), so any additional services must be agreed upon and charged for. And any construction management company should avoid work on a contingency basis.

QUALITY

A construction management company's high standard of quality will be reflected not only in its building projects but also in grammatical letters, clear reports, and neat offices. The value of quality is that if you have a reputation for it, the employees and clients that you want will more than likely want you.

Misconceptions about quality can sabotage a CM firm that sincerely wants to do good work. Here are four of the most common.

1 *Professional sophistication means quality.* Not always. Talented and dedicated professionals have been known to fixate on a narrow concept of quality. Often a professional who gains knowledge and expertise in a special field loses perspective and forgets how the profession relates to others. An architect may pursue pure aesthetics; a structural engineer may insist on a hyperbolic paraboloid when a waffle slab will do; a mechanical engineer may specify needlessly sophisticated control systems; a construction manager may concentrate on time and money at the expense of design. That's tunnel vision. Concepts of quality must reflect the broad needs of clients and the people who use the buildings.

2 *Good work starts with good workers.* There's no guarantee that this is true. Each of us has failed or

been caught in no-win situations. And sometimes great work comes from ordinary people.

Good work starts with management. Management must establish a quality-consciousness and provide corporate support. In construction management, that support includes systematic problem solving, intensive project initiation, audits, and closeouts, and education on the use of construction management systems. These procedures must be organized, enforced, and monitored from the top.

3 *Quality costs more.* Not in a business where quality means performance. There it's the lack of quality that costs. The premium for CM Inc.'s professional liability insurance equals about one-fifth of the company's profits. In most companies, approximately half of top-management energy is spent fighting brush fires started by poor work. A lot of production time and money are devoted to doing things over again.

One of our recent in-house surveys showed that the way our officers ranked a project's outcome had a direct correlation with its financial success. We were using an on-time, in-budget project and a satisfied client as criteria; the figures showed that the ones we rated as reputational failures showed poor profitability as well. So not only did we jeopardize our image on the bad jobs, but we also lost time and money. In our case, *poor* quality cost more.

Associated with this "cost equals quality" concept is the notion that quality can be ensured by loading a job with manpower. Wrong. A team that is larger than it needs to be is sloppy and ineffective. Our experience has shown that the best work comes from a lean team.

4 *Quality takes longer*. Sometimes true, but more often it is an excuse for procrastination. More good work is produced from pressure than from loose schedules. The busiest people do the best work.

Industrial managers are not as confused about quality as professionals are. In the industrial world, quality is defined as *conformance to requirements*. A worker who substitutes one material or one process for another may in fact produce a superior product but has not conformed to requirements and has circumvented quality control. A manufacturer can't let the quality of the product be left to the workers' individual concepts of quality.

Construction managers approach excellence by consistently fulfilling the obligations of their contracts, and that's a form of conformance to requirements. But the construction management definition of quality must go beyond satisfaction of a minimum standard. CM people are not assembly-line workers; they're professionals who must have the latitude to adjust the company's services to suit a project's unique needs. They must judge when to innovate, to shoot for spectacular performance, or to expand a client's view of what is attainable. And the contracts that spell out requirements for CM services are general, lacking the detail to set a clear specification for quality.

Furthermore, construction management professionals' concept of quality must include commitment and answerability to peers, stockholders, the environment, cultural values, clients, and themselves. Fortunately these commitments can be mutually supportive; in fact, often a failure to live up to one of these commitments will make it harder to live up to the others.

Example: We have had several project managers with single-minded dedication to their project. They were perfectionists; they were also unbearable to work for. Their inability to build a good team hurt the projects. Another example: If in the process of serving one client you get a reputation for bid shopping among contractors, chances are you won't get a good price for the next. You haven't lived up to your commitment, a commitment of honesty and straightforwardness with the people in your industry.

In order to nurture quality work, a company has to back up its people. It needs systems to comb through operations and isolate problems so management can correct them. The company leaders must define what good work is; they have to set and expect consistent standards of performance. But setting company standards doesn't mean insisting on "doing it the company way." The definition of quality must constantly evolve so that a company can continue to improve and respond to the special needs of each job.

Steps to Achieve Quality

Here are some steps toward achieving quality in a construction management firm.

1 *Define quality.* It's difficult to produce quality if you don't know what it is. CM companies have a responsibility to their clients and the individuals who manage their projects to provide a standard of excellence. But quality differs from project to project. It takes intellectually honest, disciplined, and analytical people to establish what quality means both within the company and for each project. Company leaders should set project goals, communicate company standards, and make sure that both are respected by everyone.

2 *Demand the best from yourself; expect it from others.* Most people who do good work don't do it because

they're smarter than other people. They excel because they want to, because it is expected of them, or because they want to set a good example. Motivation produces quality work and quality work produces motivation. You can watch this cycle at work in others.

3 *Find quality clients who want quality projects.* Part of the pleasure of working for a quality company is dealing with first-class people and projects. Being part of an elite group inspires outstanding performance.

4 *Help architects help clients.* Too often construction managers compete with the architect on a project. Quibbling destroys teamwork and hurts everyone's performance. And clients don't want to referee the people they're paying to advise them.

Construction managers can't limit their ambitions to the technical tasks in the contract. It's assumed that a construction manager's job is cost and schedule control and that quality control is the architect's responsibility. Nonsense. Both the architect and the construction manager are hired to satisfy the client's goals, which means supporting good design and the architect in every way possible.

5 *Follow through on plans and directions.* When you ask someone to do something, make sure it gets done. If you forget or neglect to call for the finished product, people may assume it wasn't important. They might take the same attitude about your next request.

6 *Avoid being trapped by "either-or."* Often an employee will present you with two unacceptable alternatives: "We either have to slip the schedule or do

bad work." Many times a feigned either-or situation is chased with something like, "I can't spend any more time on this; I'm too busy." In these cases, pull rank. Send people back to search for acceptable alternatives.

7 *Schedule time for "redos."* For repetitious tasks, simple systems can be developed to produce the right result the first time, every time. But when there's a new procedure, a special report, schedule, or study, you have to expect error, failure, or defects. How many times have you finished a job and thought, "If I could just do that over again I'd do it a lot better"? Schedule time for the redo on first-time efforts.

8 *Improve the firm with each project.* Each job can be programmed to make a professional as well as financial contribution. Each can be a step to a stronger company. Plan innovation on every project: it will produce growth, profit, and pride.

9 *Keep project-oriented.* Most people don't find inspiration in contracts, systems, and companies. They make their commitments to projects, people, and ideas. A staff will work hard to be part of a good project, but it doesn't like to be thought of as part of a production crew. The solution is to organize around *projects* rather than *functions* and to keep the whole project team informed of the project's progress.

10 *Keep bureaucracy pruned.* With time and growth a company develops bureaucratic flab. Every time a

problem arises, a procedure is created to ward off a "next time," and before long the procedures are the problem.

HARD WORK

If you work hard you will achieve more, gain more responsibility, be paid more, earn more respect, and be happier. The people who get ahead are those who do more than what's necessary—and keep on doing it. Every great leader and doer I've known has been, above all, a relentless, tireless worker. There's no way to make it to the top of any company, or stay there, on 40 hours a week—especially in the construction management business, where a smooth-running project depends on an enormous amount of behind-the-scenes planning and attention to detail.

But we all have families, houses, church activities, intellectual pursuits, hobbies, sports, and recreational interests, and these are the very important parts of a whole person. Extensive overtime dulls productivity and dampens enthusiasm. So where is the balance? Here are some thoughts.

1 *Know when to work more.* Routine tasks should be taken care of during the 40-hour week, and there's no point in increasing the volume of ordinary work. Energy is an investment. It should be used to produce the exceptional result, to work on a special project that will help the company or develop a new skill, or to meet an important deadline. Overtime should be goal-oriented time, dedicated to a specific improvement in quality or to innovation.

2 *Keep work fun.* Companies will have people who like to work hard if they like the work. You can keep people enthusiastic by creating an atmosphere of and rewarding intellectual vigor, innovation, and quality work. There's a balance in workload too: Overstaffing means boredom for hard workers, understaffing mean frustration.

3 *Set examples.* The most valuable advice a leader can give an employee is a good example. Taking the pay and prestige of leadership means you have to deliver more. Managers have to work harder to gear up, establish momentum, set examples, and train new people. Leaders have to set direction and persuade others to join their movement. During the rapid growth years at CM Inc., our officers averaged 30 percent overtime, developing new projects and following through on old ones.

4 *Avoid moonlighting.* Companies are always looking for people to groom for leadership positions. Extra effort should be invested in developing a career path, not in producing short-range income.

5 *Take vacations anyway.* The company pays you to take a vacation every year and refresh yourself. You're cheating the company, and probably yourself, if you spend the time doing chores at home. Go—there is never a good time. And come back full of ideas and enthusiasm.

THE CORPORATE CULTURE

A company is a culture, a group of people acting with similar purpose for at least 8 hours a day. You want employees who believe that they have a good place to work and good people to work with. If a company's leaders choose officers who share their values, and the officers ask the same from the people who work for them, chances are there will be a good, supportive atmosphere in the office.

1   *Collaborate.* We are at our best when we integrate our strengths, and it's important to choose people who have strengths that exceed your own. Don't be afraid to recognize them for it: collaboration should be initiated by the person who needs help. And the most successful people are those who get the best help.

    When you are looking for creative collaboration, don't overstructure meetings. A chairman who squelches arguments might as well distribute memos. It might not hurt to encourage a little controversy now and then if things get dull.

2   *Keep the company friendly.* It's a sure sign of insecurity if a middle manager makes an employee afraid to talk to the company's senior officials. Vertical friendships are important to a company. Managers should promote good relations between their teams and the boss.

    I've heard people say that it's a mistake for a manager to be friends with subordinates. I don't believe that. The closer friendships are, the better people can work together, and the more they will enjoy it. It is possible to have friends and also to have the intellectual and emotional strength to stay objective and make good business decisions. Furthermore, friendship promotes loyalties and the pooling of individual strengths. The place to draw the line? Probably at the office door.

Over the years I've come to the conclusion that office parties usually do more harm than good.

One way to keep the company friendly is to keep communications personal. This means minimizing the use of photocopies, computer printouts, word processors, and all forms of automated verbosity. And maximizing face-to-face discourse, objective debate, and creative collaboration. "Brief" and "personal" are the qualities to strive for in all interoffice communications.

While it may not seem friendly or a good way to stimulate open relationships, managers should encourage their employees to be open about their objections. The thing to watch for in heated conversations is anger that never clearly identifies its source and disintegrates into people-related—rather than issue-related—arguments.

We all fly off the handle sometimes, but if you, as a manager, abuse someone, be quick to apologize clearly and publicly. There's no room for grudges or backstabbing in a service business. Anger can, on occasion, be the only appropriate reaction to a situation, but *uncontrolled* anger is never a useful management tool.

3 *Balance leadership with participative management.* Although democracy works for government, it's too slow for a profit-oriented company. Leadership must be exercised to pull a company together; occasionally officers must throw their weight around to get things moving. The thing to watch out for is leadership by executive decree. I was once accused of having a "whim of iron." That's not exactly an open-management concept.

Participative management requires stronger leadership than an autocratic organization. You must be prepared to ask for opinions and follow them with a counterdecision. You must encourage challenge by subordinates. But remember, you are a manager because someone thinks your judgment is superior. If managers betray their own judgment to satisfy popular opinion, they aren't doing their job.

In participative management, managers treat people as equals and respect the ideas of juniors. Use a subordinate's idea even if you think it is only as good as yours. With pride of authorship, the subordinate will implement a plan of action more enthusiastically.

Be quick to lose arguments to subordinates. It's not only fair, it encourages their participation and develops their self-confidence. When you do disagree with a junior employee, avoid a lengthy discussion designed to "handle" him or her. The employee will know what you're doing and resent it. If you are going to do it your way anyhow, don't pretend you are open to suggestion, but take a minute to explain why you made that decision. Don't leave someone feeling that the effort is futile.

4   *Avoid renting people.* Once CM Inc. farmed out a team to an international company for a housing job; then we lost touch with the project. The result was that of all the good people we started with on that project, most became disgruntled and left us. Good construction management companies take responsibility for project results; they aren't labor pools.

5   *Encourage criticism and praise.* If someone seems unhappy, the best response is to check it out. You might be able to fix it, and as we all know, happy people do

better work. CM Inc. has a policy: "Bitch up, praise down." If people can't complain to their superiors, they complain to their colleagues and support staffs, and that destroys company morale.

The distinction between critics and complainers is one of intent, and open criticism should be valued. Critics are essential to the quality of the company. When an employee points out a company weakness, take time to consider. If it's valid, admit it and then enlist that employee's aid in correcting the problem.

Now for praise. It's hard to compliment a superior without sounding obsequious. But a little objective compliment will often provide the warm-up that boss-employee relationships sometimes need. As for people working for you, your attention and sincere appreciation for work well done will go further than you think. Make praise a habit; recognize it when people are trying to please you.

6 *Keep the pyramid flat.* Middle management should be kept to a minimum to reduce overhead and increase profit. With the line people closer to top management, communication and understanding are simplified both ways—thus line people will have freer rein and managers a wider view.

7 *Work with humor.* Humor is the way healthy people deal with adversity. And construction projects have plenty of adversity. When we first started CM Inc., we had a serious problem every month or two. Now two or three a day is more the average, and, like the company, the problems are bigger. You can't let them get you down.

There is a terrific story about two of our people in the Jidda airport. Up at 5:30 in the morning to catch the

Arabian express from Riyadh, they had accomplished nothing all day (no clients in town). At 2:00 a.m. they were waiting for an 8-hour flight to London that was already 4 hours late. They had indigestion from too much Arabian coffee. They were thirsty, but there was no bottled water to be found. They had been through security three times. Finally still another delay was announced. One looked at the other and said, "Just think, some people save all their lives to travel like this."

That's the spirit.

INDEX

Guaranteed maximum price (GMP), 61–62

Hard work, improving quality through,
195–197
Heat-recovery schemes, 149
Historical budgeting, 104, 140–142
Homework for selling CM, 7–12
Horizontal purchasing, 112–113
Humor:
in selling CM services, 22, 25
value for employees, 200–201
HVAC systems, 149

Information-gathering for selling CM,
7–12
Input:
EBUDG, 146
estimating, 150–156
scheduling, 129–131
WONDR-1, 148
Inspection companies, planning work of,
87–88
Inspection of sites, 8
Institutional advertising, 33
Insurance, establishing need for,
117–118
Interview teams, 15–17
Interviews (*see* Presentations)

Jargon, avoiding use of, 22
Jobs (*see* Projects, construction)
Joint ventures, 13–14

Leadership balanced with participative
management, 198–199
Leads, qualifying, 4–7
Leave-behind material at presentations,
30–31
Legal counsel, establishing need for,
117–118
Lighting systems, 149
Liquidated-damages clauses, 98
Listening and learning during homework
stage, 11–12
Long-lead items, purchasing, 113
LUMEN II program, 149
Lump-sum competitive bidding, 58

Lump-sum design-build contracts, 64–65

Management:
expense (cost), 187–189
growth, 173–180
middle, minimizing, 201
participative, 198–199
project, 78–89
salary, 180–187
(*See also entries beginning with term:*
CM)
Management plans as criterion for awarding
contracts, 49
Managers, construction (*see* Construction
managers)
Managing CM companies, 169–201
(*See also* CM companies)
Manpower versus time available in design
schedules, 96, 97
Market analyses, 111–112
Master schedules, 95, 96
Middle management, minimizing, 201
Momentum, establishing, 87
Monitoring permits, 118
Monitoring project schedules, 94–95
Monitoring as step in project management,
79, 88–89
Monthly reports, 89, 92
Multiple contracts:
with fast-track, questions about, 29
with traditional scheduling, 74–75

Network diagrams, 93–94, 137–138

Occupancy schedules, 101, 103
Open bids, 49–50
Operations, reasons for importance of, 4
Organization:
of client companies, project delivery
strategies influenced by, 45
of CM companies, 171–173
Organization charts, 86–87, 171–173
Organizing as step in project management,
78, 85–88
Output:
EBUDG, 146
estimating, 158–162
scheduling, 131–140

ABOUT
THE
AUTHOR

Charles B. Thomsen, FAIA, is currently President and Chief Executive Officer of The CRS Group, Inc., Houston, Texas, one of the world's largest architectural engineering and construction management companies. Previously, he was President, Chairman, and CEO of CM, Inc., the construction management subsidiary of The CRS Group. Under his direction, CM, Inc. grew from its founding in 1971 to an international company handling some $12 billion worth of construction in the U.S. and around the world.

Mr. Thomsen holds degrees in architecture from the University of Oklahoma and from M.I.T. He lectures frequently at universities and seminars, he is an adjunct professor at Rice University, and he has written many articles, studies, and reports on construction management, architecture, and construction.